The Challenge of Greatness

The Legacy of Great Teachers

Michael D. Gose

ROWMAN & LITTLEFIELD EDUCATION
A division of
ROWMAN & LITTLEFIELD PUBLISHERS, INC.
Lanham • New York • Toronto • Plymouth, UK

KH

Published by Rowman & Littlefield Education
A division of Rowman & Littlefield Publishers, Inc.
A wholly owned subsidiary of The Rowman & Littlefield Publishing Group, Inc.
4501 Forbes Boulevard, Suite 200, Lanham, Maryland 20706
www.rowman.com

10 Thornbury Road, Plymouth PL6 7PP, United Kingdom

British Library Cataloguing in Publication Information Available

Library of Congress Cataloging-in-Publication Data

Gose, Michael D. (Michael Douglas), 1946- author.
The challenge of greatness : the legacy of great teachers / Michael D. Gose.
p. cm.
Includes bibliographical references and index.
ISBN 978-1-61048-089-5 (cloth : alk. paper) -- ISBN 978-1-61048-090-1 (pbk. : alk. paper) -- ISBN
978-1-61048-091-8 (electronic)
1. Teachers. 2. Effective teaching. I. Title.
LB1775.G67 2012
371.1--dc23

2012014048

Printed in the United States of America

6/28/13

The first thing to know about great teachers is that they are, in the best way, unorthodox. Great teachers' methods and intuitions are different. They don't operate like other teachers, and they don't believe everything they're taught or told. They work by instinct more than even they know, having worked out the strategies and approaches that succeed for them in reaching different students. In an extraordinarily high number of cases, their instincts lead them to the results they want—better-educated students.

—Rosanne Liesveld and Jo Ann Miller

Contents

Acknowledgments

I dedicate this book to my granddaughter, Sia Day Kresch, who brings immeasurable joy, and for whom I hope has many great teachers.

The prospects of having five students whom I had previously had in Pepperdine University's Great Books Colloquium take my Teacher Education, Curriculum and Methods course toward their becoming teachers themselves was the direct inspiration for the work that I did that led to this book. In fact, I had recruited only one of the five for my class. I had recommended that Kanako Suzuki and Brendan Fereday apply to the same Stanford University Teacher Education program that I had attended many years earlier. I encouraged Megan Reel to join the Peace Corps; Chelsea Reimert to become a lawyer; and Katherine Sexton, whom I had known since her birth, I had undoubtedly given her subtle and not-so-subtle hints that I hoped she would take this class with me.

Any or all of the five may choose careers outside of teaching, but if any of these five become teachers, I have every expectation that they will be great teachers, so much so that I reenvisioned how I wanted to teach the Curriculum and Methods class that I have been teaching for over thirty years. Even though I could not anticipate how other students in the course might respond to the materials that ended up in this book, I had an unusually good sense of what might well serve these five students with whom I had already established the teacher-student, students-teachers relationship.

I argue in this book that no teacher needs to take on the challenge of greatness. Good teaching is good. Garfield High School students did not have to take Jaime Escalante's Advanced Placement Calculus course, but once enrolled, they had a clear and external standard to meet and the need for an especially great teacher.

Students who enroll in Teacher Education and the Curriculum and Methods course do not have to commit to being great teachers to be important contributors to their future students' education. Thus, as I finish the manuscript for this book, I am keenly aware of the challenge to teach a course in which all students will not necessarily want or choose to rise to the challenge of the Great Teachers as first identified by Houston Peterson in his 1946 book, *Great Teachers*. While my own class will be a lab to work out the challenges to my own teaching, the inspiration that Kanako, Megan, Chelsea, Katherine, and Brendan provided accounts for the impulse to create this book. I thank them.

I am especially indebted to my editor, Tom Koerner, for his ongoing support of this study; Lauren Batterham, for her work on the manuscript; Michelle Grue, for her thoughtful review of the text; and Erin Shitama for her help in conceptualizing the book's overall approach.

I am delighted to recognize the following teachers whom the author did not study but believes to be great: Verne Riggle, Pat Cairns, Betty Glass, Gary Hart, Victoria Myers, Damian Jenkins, Caleb Clanton, Mason Marshall, Jesse Covington, Bob Sexton, Dan Caldwell, Joi Carr, Michio Nagai, Carrol Pitts, Joe Randazzo, Patricia Aboud, Bob Clement, Jeannie Spitler, Peter Tracey, Art Walsh, Monty Steadman, Kris Stewart, Chris Grimm, Kris Janati, Hannah Punzalan Housley, Charlene Mello, Nick Leon, Paul Begin, Tanja Carter, Alex Diener, David Holmes, Dan Fader, John Flaherty, Frank Cruz, Claudette Wilson, Jim McGoldrick, JoAnn Taylor, Bob Escudero, Lisa Kodama, Carrie Wall, Monica Duran, Russell Lee-Sung, Bob King, Maria King, Mark Mallinger, Dick Tingey, Henry Rubio, Ken Montgomery, Becky Heino, Anne Perez, Kim Logan, and Vito Perrone.

Foreword

Teaching is an art, not a science. Good teaching is a gift, not a learned skill. Great teaching is a calling, not a job. In striving for greatness, mentors matter. As teachers, we can all learn from great teachers. *The Challenge of Greatness* is a compendium of advice and examples from great teachers distilled by a senior professor who has sought to emulate them in his own teaching and distill their experiences. I know of no better way to introduce this book than to consider how one of my own greatest teachers personified the characteristics of great teachers listed in this book.

Some people mistakenly believe that great scholars cannot be great teachers because they are too smart to relate to their students or too busy with their scholarship to care about teaching. This is simply false. Some of the greatest scholars are also the most inspiring classroom instructors. The legendary biologist Edward O. Wilson, who transformed our understanding of social insects and human behavior, also regularly filled the largest lecture halls at Harvard for his introductory classes and received prizes for undergraduate (as well as graduate) instruction. Although tempted to write about Wilson, as a graduate student at Harvard, I was only an observer in Wilson's undergraduate classes and never had him as my instructor. For my undergraduate mentor, I turn instead to a similarly renowned scholar and teacher, Williams College's celebrated political scientist and pioneer in leadership studies James McGregor Burns.

By the time I entered Williams College – a school then known more for its teaching than for its scholarship – Burns was clearly the school's foremost scholar. He had received the Pulitzer Prize in biography and the National Book Award in history for his classic two-volume biography of Franklin Delano Roosevelt, been awarded the bronze star and four battle awards for his service as a combat historian during World War Two, served as the president of the American Political Science Association, and been a Democratic candidate for the U.S. House of Representatives. Nevertheless, true to the Williams tradition, Burns was a teacher first. Further, and perhaps most remarkably given Williams' isolated location, Burns stressed the practical aspects of political science and leadership skills. Keeping one eye fixed on the community in which we live, he examined how political leaders impacted actual lives and how politicians could transform society through moral leadership.

Like so many great teachers, Professor Burns led by inspiring emulation. In the classroom, he did not instruct and tell students what they should know so much as he suggested and let them realize what they think. Despite his thorough knowledge of the course subject matter – after all, he virtually invented it as a modern academic discipline – Professor Burns did not seek to overawe his students with his formal knowledge or many distinctions. Instead, he drew on a rich fund of examples and stories from his own life and those of the American politicians that he had studied, particularly FDR, to explore the ideas of political leadership that was the topic of our course. I took Professor Burns' class in the mid-1970s after I had already decided that preppy Williams was not the college for me – a public-school product from the Midwest farm belt – and had been admitted as a transfer student to the University of Michigan beginning the next semester. For my last term at Williams, as a rising sophomore, I decided to take Professor Burns' senior leadership course. My idea was to go for the best, no matter what it cost me in my grade, because the grade no longer really mattered. I was the only sophomore in the course. Most of my classmates were senior political science majors.

From the very first, Professor Burns was an inspiration. In my own quest for an undergraduate major, I had already abandoned political science for history due to the excess of model building in the political science courses that I had taken. Here was Professor Burns, president of the Political Science Association, and clearly the most respected scholar at Williams, telling us about American political leadership through stories, anecdotes, and history. He even confided in me one day, as I explained (at his request) my decision to leave Williams and political science, that he would have opted for history over political science if he had anticipated the turns those fields would take. He invited me to his home for Thanksgiving dinner when he found out that I would remain in Williamstown during the holiday break.

Professor Burns welcomed the entire class into his home to watch the 1972 election returns, at which time he claimed victory because of George McGovern's local win in Massachusetts and predicted that "the crows would come home to roost during Nixon's second term." As the Watergate scandal unfolded over the coming months, we would learn just how right Burns was about Richard Nixon. Moral and ethical leadership did matter – just as Burns had told us – and Nixon failed us all on these vital points even though he initially was an effective transactional president. During the entire election night, between fielding calls from the national media for comment, Burns talked freely to each of us about the American electoral process and never shied away from sharing his political passion for liberal, values-based democracy. His enthusiasm for practical politics and for broadening American democratic values as encapsulated in Roosevelt's Four Freedoms Speech – freedom of speech, freedom of worship, freedom from want, freedom from fear – was contagious. This night further helped to dispel the insulation between teacher and student that hobbles so much of higher education. Ensuing classes became increasingly rich exchanges of insights and ideas. As students, our respect for our teacher grew with familiarity.

I was living in Ann Arbor by the time that Professor Burns had finished grading my final paper for that fall course. It arrived full of insightful comments and carried the highest grade that I had yet received at Williams. Both provided further inspiration for me, no longer even a student at his school. But I soon received a call from a Williams' admission counselor who had spoken with Professor Burns and I ended up returning to Williams for my senior year and then going on to graduate school in history, as Professor Burns advised. When I was surprised by word of having won the Pulitzer Prize for a book that dealt with 20th Century American political leadership, my first thought was that Professor Burns had also received that award for such a book. I was in good company indeed. Professor Burns had cared about me and my development, just as he had cared about each of his students, and aroused in me the sort of critical, independent, and values-based thinking that he had exemplified in his own teaching and scholarship. By challenging his students to greatness, James McGregor Burns left the legacy of a great teacher. As you read this insightful book, I hope that you (like me) will reflect on your own greatest teachers and deepen your appreciation for what it means to be challenged by greatness and called to be a great teacher.

— Edward J. Larson
Pepperdine University

Preface: The Author's Indebtedness to His Own Great Teachers

This book seeks to recognize the legacy of great teachers and especially the great teachers with whom I had the great fortune of having studied. The august group includes Advanced Placement and Honors high school teachers Alice Coleman and John M. Daly; Coach Paul Beck; college professors Lewis Owen and Royce Clark; university professors Frank Hawkinshire, Fannie Shaftel, Arturo Pacheco, Elizabeth Traugott, Elliot Eisner, Elizabeth Cohen, and David Tyack. Very different personalities; all are great teachers.

I believe that my own students have benefited from my aspirations to be such a teacher as the above-mentioned ones, regardless of whatever excellence I may have or may not have established in my own teacher-student to students-teachers relationships. Now near the end of my career, I would like somehow to pass on the mantle that implicitly challenges members of the next generation to join the ranks to be one of the next great teachers.

In this study, I will reference Jaime Escalante perhaps the most often for particular examples. This is because he is perhaps the best-known American great teacher of this past generation, and much about him is still available and can still be gained from watching the film *Stand and Deliver* and by reading Jay Mathews's book, *Escalante: The Best Teacher in America*. I will also use the teachers from another recent Jay Mathews book about teachers, *Work Hard. Be Nice.: How Two Inspired Teachers Created the Most Promising Schools in America*, particularly the teacher, Rafe Esquith. Esquith influenced Mathews's story, and he has also written his own books about teaching that have been recent best sellers and are also readily available.

But Coleman, Daly, Beck, Owen, Clark, Hawkinshire, Shaftel, Traugott, Cohen, Eisner, Pacheco, and Tyack most inform this book. They are the truest reality checks on whether what I have written is timely, meaningful, and true. Hopefully, but not inevitably, the reader has had the good fortune of having his/her life touched by such a teacher.

When I once worked in a jail setting I would sometimes ask if any of the inmates had had a great teacher. I never had any of the inmates indicate that he had even had a favorite teacher. The world could only be a better place with the exposure of every student to great teachers somewhere along the way. However, despite the self-reports of those inmates, I nevertheless suspect that examples of great teachers are more plentiful than perhaps usually imagined, partially because of the possibility that when a lesson needs to be learned, the teacher will appear. Perhaps this book in its own small way may nudge a few more teachers toward the commitments to greatness (and the concomitant acceptance of the failures that litter its way).

Introduction

A PRELIMINARY NOTE

Great teacher candidate readers of this book—you are most likely looking herein for whatever you need, and only what you might need, to be great. In doing so, you ought to be extremely selective. The best "exam" on how well you read this book will not be whether you can remember and use all of its parts but whether you found anything that might make a difference for you in becoming one of the great teachers. This book recommends what Elliot Eisner describes as "expressive outcomes." I hope that you will find, retain, and express an outcome that will make this reading worthwhile.

CHAPTER SUMMARIES

Chapter 1 describes a pantheon of thirty-two great teachers who were studied for insight into how great teachers are different from others and what they do to be great teachers.

Chapter 2 offers Houston Peterson's analysis of Great Teachers' characteristics as a way of considering how great teachers are perceived and described.

Chapter 3 considers how great teachers go about achieving their reputations for greatness. Great teachers set high standards, develop a great teacher persona, use the curriculum to expand students' views of education, use the hidden curriculum to teach students responsibility, establish relationships with the students, use the classroom as a lab to discover what works best with these students, and create a sense of community. Great teachers are more, not

1

less, susceptible to failure, because they take risks so that they can learn from mistakes, and while never comfortable with failure, they embrace it as a requisite for having long-term success with students.

Chapter 4 offers a myriad of considerations that might help the great teacher identify factors and approaches for working successfully with each and every student in an individual classroom. "Appreciating differences; diversifying instruction" are watchwords for the great teacher. The considerations of this chapter might, emphasis *might*, help identify possibilities that will help match the particular class with each individual student.

The chapter includes frequently perceived differences among students that may or may not fit the unique individuals within a teacher's particular class, a range of potential teaching strategies, and a few considerations of how great teachers may surpass excellence. The chapter is premised on an understanding that "differential effects" warn teachers that what may be best practices for most students in most places are not necessarily what will work best with a particular student or class.

Chapter 5 warns that great teaching causes greater challenges and has greater costs than good teaching.

Chapter 6 posits that without first confronting the factors that keep teachers from being great teachers, the discussion about being a great teacher is moot. Certainly all teachers need to know how to manage a classroom, but those are learnable skills by anyone willing to take responsibility for a classroom. The great challenge for prospective great teachers will be to face the uncomfortable ways that one's biography, which led to a decision to teach, will also limit the vision of teaching without a concerted willingness to understand how one's strengths are also usually one's weaknesses. Reasonably sure of self-identity, the challenge for teachers is to open up to all their students' quite different value systems, something that those who think of themselves as well raised often find difficult to do.

Chapter 7 concludes with the challenge of the great teachers' legacy to be good, teach great. All of the chapters are dedicated to the great teachers and with the hope that others will take up the quest to be a great teacher as a continuing legacy for subsequent generations.

The Appendix includes caveats about the limitations of this study, clarifications about its implicit and explicit biases, and a review of other perspectives on great teachers and great teaching that compare and contrast with that of this study.

Chapter One

A Pantheon of Great Teachers

> The first thing to know about great teachers is that they are, in the best way, unorthodox. Great teachers' methods are different. They don't operate like other teachers, and they don't believe everything they're taught or told. They work by instinct more than even they know, having worked out the strategies and approaches that succeed for them in reaching different students. In an extraordinarily high number of cases, their instincts lead them to the results they want—better educated students.
>
> —Rosanne Liesveld and Jo Ann Miller

Liesveld and Miller open the conversation about great teachers. Great teachers are unorthodox. The cinematic image of a great teacher like Edward James Olmos' teacher in the film, *Stand and Deliver*, is based on the reality of famed calculus teacher, Jaime Escalante. Olmos captured specific idiosyncratic Escalante characteristics, including his speech patterns and gestures as well as the Escalante admonition for his students to have *ganas*, a determined will to succeed.

No other great teacher would be unorthodox in the same way as Escalante, but a single great teacher might very well stand before his students in a chef's hat and apron, with a huge cleaver in hand, and chop an apple into fractions before an audience of stunned and progressively less recalcitrant math students.

Great teachers' methods and intuitions are different. Apparently a great teacher as well as a great poet, there is a story that poet and English professor Theodore Roethke crawled into his classroom from the snow and from the second-story window ledge and declared to his students that "the cardinal sin of an educator is to be boring."

Great teachers do not operate like other teachers, and they do not believe everything that they are taught or told. Princeton educated, former marine colonel, and Advanced Placement History teacher, John M. Daly, required his public school students to buy their own individual copies of a college history text, T. A. Bailey's *The American Pageant*, so that he would not have to use the inferior, but provided, high school text. Daly assured his reluctant students that, indeed, he knew this was against the law, but what were they going to do about it?

Great teachers work by instinct and work out strategies and approaches to be successful with different students. In the film *To Sir, with Love*, Sidney Poitier, portraying real-life teacher E. R. Braithwaite, takes a stack of outdated classroom texts and dumps them into the classroom trash can, and then he tells his class that they will soon graduate and that they are ill equipped for the life that will soon confront them.

> Braithwaite: "That's it! Those are out. They are useless to you. I realized you are not children. You will be adults in a few weeks, with all the responsibilities."
> Student: "What are we going to talk about, Sir?"
> Braithwaite: "About life . . . survival . . . love . . . death, sex, marriage . . . rebellion, anything you want."
> Student: "I never did see one like him."

Such differences and unorthodoxy among great teachers inspire their students. But what do such great teachers look like in greater detail, and what sort of things do they do specifically to achieve great teaching?

XXXII (32) GREAT TEACHERS

> Decades of research have proven that talents are extremely powerful, and the influence of teaching with strengths on students has a dramatic long-term effect.
> —Rosanne Liesveld and Jo Ann Miller (2005:13)

Thus, this study "knows" that statement above about the importance of teaching to be true, so it explores the characteristics of great teachers and how they may have gotten that way. Here starts the list of the thirty-two (XXXII) immortals; they are not ranked in competition with each other.

History teacher John Daly and English teacher Alice Coleman combined forces to create a two-year Advanced Placement and Honors English and history program that would prepare their students for the selective colleges and universities. The pair: so different, so alike.

Mission Bay High School Advanced Placement and Honors English teacher, Alice Coleman (I), was a lady without that term being a pejorative one, and if the term *lady* has fallen into disrepute at least in some circles because of concerns such as the prospect that ladies might not be tough enough to be CEOs, this literate, well-dressed woman who wore pearls to teach was someone to contend with and whom her students, and presumably all others, would not want to mess with. (Although she would not appreciate the ending of the previous sentence with a preposition, Professor Elizabeth Traugott might observe that since it ends the sentence, it is thus used as an adverb.)

Curiously, Coleman's partner in the Humanities Advanced Placement program at Mission Bay High School, John M. Daly (II), seemed even more daunting, yet was in fact the teacher with whom students did spar. Daly thrived on conflict and competition—never in an overtly friendly way, but eventually not beyond what a student could endure, as Daly roused students to exceed their own limited self-expectations. A Princeton man and former marine colonel beloved by his alumni, but never with what commonly is called affection.

Physical Education teacher and sometimes basketball coach, Paul Beck (III), was the most respected person at Mission Bay High School. When Beck's name failed to appear in *What It Means to Be a Teacher*, Tom Goodwin wrote a quick note, "What about Beck?" Beck engaged all of his students, wanting them to be, and helping them to be, better, and all that that might entail.

Occidental College English literature professor Lewis Owen (IV) had the twinkle in his eye. Reportedly at the time of his own PhD degree, only two Americans a year were admitted to the University of London's doctoral program in literature, and he had been one of those two. Whether that story was true or not—print the legend. His English, red, academic robe, and round instead of pointed academic hat, led generations of students to suspect that academia was also great theater and further inspired them to graduate work so that they, too, could wear such a costume of distinction. Erudite, witty, he had a way of cocking his head and looking into his discussant's eyes such that when he spoke that person might very well feel she or he had been speaking to a cardinal, a pope, a saint. His students wanted to be so cultured, and to please him.

Pepperdine University's religion professor, Royce Clark (V), had a way of making familiar material seem fresh. Soft-spoken, a clear and direct communicator, somehow he made a conversation come alive and animated with a wealth of ideas, perspectives, and new understandings.

Stanford University sociologist and educator Frank Hawkinshire (VI) intentionally raised the anxiety level of his Stanford students beyond what any outside observer would likely think a good idea. He marched into each class precisely on time with three to five teaching assistants following dutifully behind him, perhaps like General Patton occupying yet another unfriendly enemy city. Hawkinshire expected his students to learn to think like sociologists, including making their own observations about his classroom dynamics.

Working with the class's learning teams, he was so astute about group dynamics that he seemed to have been to the small study group's work meetings. For a final exam he might have the class play a game, like Capture the Flag on a playground, and then have each student write a separate analysis of the group dynamics. All "outside of the box," eye-opening, academic education. Students learned to use theory and research toward coming to their individual insights and critiques.

At least some of Stanford University linguistic teacher Elizabeth Traugott's (VII) students thought that she deserved to be teaching even better students than the highly competitive students that she had. Extremely intellectual, absolutely brilliant, but also surprisingly savvy. When a group of master degree students thought that they had beaten her very demanding system by enrolling in her class as credit/no credit, Traugott came to realize what she was up against, and then mentioned one day in class that, of course, students would have to earn the equivalent of a "B" to receive that credit since that was the only grade that was truly passing in graduate school. Was that "just" on her part? It was certainly shrewd, and those students raised their level of performance, and all did pass.

Elizabeth Cohen (VIII) used her research on behalf of creating a more democratic society. She worked to forestall the effects of "diffuse status characteristics" (read *prejudice*) by teaching lower-social-status students something that higher-status students would want to learn from them. She was also thought to be the most conscientious about making sure that all of her students finished their programs and degrees.

Stanford's Elliot Eisner (IX), author of such books as *The Enlightened Eye* and *The Educational Imagination*, explained to students that his early work as a painter informed his ideas about education. In response to a classroom request for students to use a metaphor to describe an educational insight, one student observed that as a teacher Dr. Eisner thought of himself as a classical musician; his ideas were so discordant with what else was going on in professional education that his teaching was heard by students as if he was playing acid rock; the truer metaphor, however, was jazz, as he created and recreated his thinking as he interacted with his students. Eminent in his field and an inspiration to his students.

When Stanford School of Education graduate students felt overwhelmed, they looked for, and usually readily found, professor Arturo Pacheco (X). A former Peace Corps volunteer, he constantly had students into his home on campus, seemed to reside during the day in the school's hallways talking with individual and small groups of students. His was one of the early voices of the richness of cultural pluralism (and its advantages for sustaining a rich and plentiful life). He argued that America was not a melting pot, but more like a tossed salad, with each group making its own unique contribution to the whole. Like all great teachers he opened students to a much larger world.

Stanford educator Fannie Shaftel (XI) was thought by her students to be the best person on the planet. She developed "role-playing for social values," a powerful methodology for helping students develop the understanding and learn the skills for responsible social choices. If talking to Lewis Owen was like talking to a saint, Shaftel must be likened to an angel. During times of exigency, Stanford students might well complain about any and all other demanding professors, but Shaftel was sacred and beyond any voiced student criticism. She was uniquely able to accept students as they were while communicating to them a sense of what they could become.

Historian and educator, Stanford's David Tyack (XII) won Teacher of the Year awards most years. Without being notably charismatic. Rode his bike. Brought his dog to school (which was against the rules, of course, but who would think to enforce them against the incredibly responsible David Tyack?). The dog sat quietly with him in his office during his frequent meetings with students, somehow reassuring said students that there was life beyond the Stanford library. Many of his classes met at his home, and perhaps all of his classes were invited into his home. He used a wide variety of teaching methods to keep his students interested. He taught his students how to do and appreciate history.

Tyack concerned himself with students' performances more than his own. As many articles and books as he wrote, he probably wrote more words in student recommendations. He gave students his home phone number. Advised and counseled students about school and life. Obviously loved his job, his family, his dog, his students. Deeply respected. While he did not have the quirky persona associated with other great teachers, he raised excellence to greatness. And lest the reader suspect that he belies the tendency toward insubordination that Houston Peterson associated with great teaching, keep in mind the dog.

Tyack concludes this preliminary list of great teachers to set up the contrast to a very similar teacher, also an historian, who, while excellent, was not a great teacher in the terms of this book. This excellent teacher, who shall remain anonymous, provides a cautionary tale, and perhaps not the expected one. "Mere" excellence deserves praise, not the following invidious comparison to greatness.

This excellent teacher had the smarts and the integrity of a Tyack. This was a teacher well regarded by her students, administrators, other teachers, and parents. But in the terms of this book's working definition of great teaching that will be developed in chapters 2 and 3, this teacher did not take on the additional commitments of developing a teaching persona, using her class as a lab, and developing a sense of a learning community.

Such undertakings required for greatness in teaching cannot, must not, be an expectation of anyone save that teacher herself. This teacher was professional and personable; she used "best practices"; she was a responsible member of her school staff. She accepted that some students would choose to fail; she did not tend to go home terribly conflicted about some school issue and was much more likely to give her family her full attention. She simply did not develop that special teaching persona/identity/character that alerted students that something special was expected. Students either responded responsibly to best practices, or did not.

Her courses were well taught; students progressed. But they did so without any sense of their being in it together toward some larger common purpose. She did not push the envelope, and yet students and her school are very lucky to have such a fine teacher. But hers is not the kind of teaching that tends to change students' lives and student aspirations. This study has great respect for all teaching, and especially excellent teaching, but it sets its focus on the even more rarefied "great teaching."

■■■

The characteristics thought to associate with great teaching must hold up under the scrutiny of individual examples. For methodology I first considered all the teachers that I had had and the extent to which any of them were arguably "great teachers." I concluded that the twelve characterized above were truly great teachers in the terms Houston Peterson established as characteristic of great teachers. I then expanded his study to those whom I had worked with, taught, observed, read about, seen as depicted on television or in movies, and read about in fictional accounts. Eventually I added twenty additional teachers for a peer group of thirty-two teachers thought to be great.

The study then focuses on this Pantheon of Great Teachers to account for how one might attempt to be one of the great teachers. The following profile of the additional twenty teachers that I added to the group completes the list of the great teachers by which to consider the characteristics of great teachers, and what those great teachers might do differently than other teachers.

Here, then, is a profile for the remaining twenty teachers (added to the twelve who were included earlier):

> Gene Bream has now been adored by a generation of middle school students. He has also been a mainstay of the Pepperdine University Teacher Education Program, serving as mentor to countless student

teachers. His students are visibly delighted to be in his class. Some of his students accompany him on a yearly summer trip to Europe. One of his most revealing practices is that he asks all of his students what resources that they might have that would enrich the next unit of study in his Social Studies program.

Jim Herndon wrote *The Way It Spozed to Be*, *How to Survive in Your Native Land*, and *Notes from a Schoolteacher*. He taught junior high school in a suburb south of San Francisco, and for many years he was the union representative for the teachers. His books were something of a bible for the Curriculum and Methods course at Pepperdine University's Seaver College. His books offer great insight into what really goes on in school.

Paulo Freire's first book, *Pedagogy of the Oppressed*, contrasts "dialogics" between the teacher-student and students-teachers with the banking concept of knowledge, where colonizing teachers make deposits of knowledge and then withdrawals at exam time. His emphasis on the transforming possibilities of education is consistent with what all great teachers work toward.

Leo Tolstoy, more famous as a Russian novelist, became a teacher in a village school, and he wrote about that experience. A precursor of open education, his regard for his own students is as exemplary as his writing.

E. R. Braithwaite evidenced great teaching in his account of *To Sir, with Love*, and Sidney Poitier certainly found those qualities of greatness in the portrayal in the film version. Braithwaite makes the cut for this list especially because of his example of accepting that what he was initially doing as a teacher was not working, that his students could learn despite the fact that they were not, and then using his class as a lab to find what would work.

Sylvia Ashton-Warner wrote books that included *Teacher*, which established the power of her work with "key vocabulary" with preschool Maori children, and then *Spearpoint*, about her struggles with urban American students.

Rafe Esquith has become perhaps the currently best-known teacher in America. His books, including *Teach Like Your Hair's on Fire*, book tours, and appearance on programs like *Oprah*, his help of the teachers of the KIPP (Knowledge Is Power Program) program, and his decades of devotion and success with students offer a wealth of opportunity for anyone to study a great teacher.

Is Gloria Ladson-Billings a great teacher? Her books are about other teachers, but her book, *Dreamkeepers*, while emphasizing "only" effective teaching, shows a concern for teachers responding to the real needs of their actual students and becoming involved in their schools' communities, proves that she has special insights that may be helpful to the teacher seeking greatness. So she becomes in the absence of documentation at least an honorary member of this Great Teachers Peer Group.

Robert Inchausti's book, *Spitwad Sutras*, is an overlooked classic, and his account of an experienced teacher, Brother Blake, may be the most revealing account of how great teachers depend upon a transcendent view of life for their motivation, support, and direction.

Jaime Escalante, the Garfield High School Advanced Placement Calculus teacher of some notoriety, was the great teacher depicted by Edward James Olmos in the very popular film, *Stand and Deliver*. He was also the subject of an outstanding book by Jay Mathews, *Escalante*. Because the film and book offer ready images by which to imagine more specifically the characteristics and practices of great teachers, they are especially emphasized in this book.

Ben Jimenez was Escalante's partner in crime and becomes perhaps the most important example for this book, *The Challenge of Greatness*. Jay Mathews documents how Jimenez started his teaching career without the basic classroom management skills, yet became a great teacher despite his otherwise shy personality. He embodies the thesis and hope that great teaching relies upon commitment rather than having been born with a charismatic personality.

Dave Levin, a founder of the KIPP schools, started his teaching career with Teach for America. Jay Mathews describes him as full of energy and more mature than his partner, Mike Feinberg, but also as annoying, aggressive, and ambitious, and describes both Levin and Feinberg as having a "fondness for putting themselves in situations for which they were ill prepared."

Mike Feinberg began with Dave Levin in the Teach for America program, and the two went on to become the cofounders of the KIPP schools. Jay Mathews describes Feinberg as talkative, full of creative ideas, as having a reputation of being an unholy nuisance, as an activist, yet also nice, funny, social, and having exceptional charm. At the beginning of his teaching career Mathews observes that Feinberg "was turning into an exceptional teacher, but it was clear to him (Feinberg) that he was not good enough." Curiously this study finds that one can probably be a great teacher prior to producing great teaching. It would seem that great teachers take on the characteristics and commitments to be great teachers, but only as their skills do improve do they become better recognized.

Harriett Ball was the mentor to Dave Levin and Mike Feinberg, the two teachers who founded the Knowledge Is Power Program (KIPP) schools. Jay Mathews describes her as having creativity, charisma, organization, timing, and absolute devotion, keeping her classroom vibrant and interesting.

Frank Corcoran, who is particularly important to the challenge of this book for a teacher to be one of the great teachers, did not have the obvious charisma of Feinberg or Levin. Yet he still went on to become a nationally recognized teacher of the year. Mathews describes Corcoran as sweet tempered, passive, self-effacing, who had initial problems with classroom discipline. The source for Corcoran's great teaching was that he had good instincts regarding children, and he was able to connect with them.

Larry Giacomino taught high school science at three different northern California high schools for over thirty years. Perhaps he is a great teacher because he is such a great learner. He is the one great teacher on the list who studied under one of the others, Joe Cattarin. Giacomino taught high school biology and chemistry, but also backpacking, mountain climbing, and ropes courses. He sought out the women's gymnastics coach to improve his climbing technique, the English teacher about Jack London, the laundry person about "good reads" in popular novels. His interest in virtually all knowledge makes for common ground with virtually all of his students.

Charles Chang Park established himself as a great middle school teacher, and then moved into school administration, now working at Jackie Robinson's former high school, John Muir High School, in Pasadena, California. "Destined" to go to UCLA as a premed student, Dr. Park elected to go to Pepperdine and pursue his quest to become a great teacher and educator.

Socrates makes the list because leaving him off would be like ignoring the five-hundred-pound gorilla in the living room. Great teachers continue to ask great questions and engage their students in dialogue to pursue yet better questions.

Pete Dixon of the television series, *Room 222*, makes the list as the fictional teacher best meeting the characteristics of great teaching delineated in this book. As argued in the book, *Sophie's World*, itself a review of Western philosophy, fictional characters have a life of their own that can sometimes be better understood and known than real people. An account of great teaching should at least pause to acknowledge the contribution of such figures as Mr. Chips, Jean Brodie, Mr. Hand, Robin Williams's portrayal of the teacher in *Dead Poet's Society*, Professor Kingsfield from *Paper Chase*, and others.

Joe Cattarin should have a statue gracing the entrance to Half Moon Bay
   High School. He was an inspirational teacher for over four decades,
   was known early in his career to have slept on the trainer's table in the
   gym's locker room some nights after a long day and prospects of an
   early school morning. He managed to maintain greatness through
   times of great social change at large and within his community, and
   did so with quality, dignity, grace, and integrity that was unassailable.
   Some years school administrators' greatest problem was what to do
   with the angry parents of students who did not manage to get scheduled into one of Mr. Cattarin's history classes.

These are the thirty-two teachers to test against our working definition of
great teachers and great teacher characteristics, a definition developed almost
entirely upon the work of Houston Peterson in his 1946 book, *Great Teachers*.

Chapter Two

How Great Teachers Are Perceived (and Described)

The first thing to know about great teachers is that they are, in the best way, unorthodox. Great teachers' methods and intuitions are different. They don't operate like other teachers, and they don't believe everything they're taught or told. They work by instinct more than even they know, having worked out the strategies and approaches that succeed for them in reaching different students. In an extraordinarily high number of cases, their instincts lead them to the results they want—better educated students.
—Rosanne Liesveld and Jo Ann Miller (2005:15)

Here is the measure/indices/device for rating great teaching. It is largely based on characteristics identified by Houston Peterson in his 1946 book, *Great Teachers*. While the device has not been tested for reliability and validity, it has sufficient prima facie validity to be useful. The device was very useful, for example, in understanding why a young, great teacher was having difficulty being accepted and recognized for such during his unsuccessful candidacy for tenure.

Peterson did not in fact create an actual list of characteristics, but he did write an epilogue to his book that summarized what he found great teachers had in common. This study cobbles together a list from Peterson's observations to help conduct an initial inquiry about great teachers, especially to understand better the conflict that great teachers often face within the school setting. Here is the working definition of the great teacher, using Peterson's own language as closely as possible to fit into such a list.

14

THE CHARACTERISTICS OF GREAT TEACHERS

Great teachers cross grade and school levels and subject matters; they do not use the same approaches to curriculum or pedagogy. But they share common characteristics in terms of the response of students, their qualities as teachers, and their interaction with students. Again, primarily on the basis of Houston Peterson's work, and as much as possible in his own words.

The characteristics of historically Great Teachers

1. Had no fear of feeling and did not attempt to achieve that specious academic objectivity that can freeze a class.
2. Had thorough knowledge of the subject, whether that means by scholarship or by personal research; an original and penetrating intelligence; played easily with facts and ideas.
3. Had a rich fund of example, metaphor, and story to make the complex more simple and to make learning meaningful.
4. Was the "best" teacher, not necessarily the most "finished" teacher, often working through ideas struggling for expression, rather than simply presenting preformulated ones; exhibited an original and penetrating intelligence at work, playing freely with facts and ideas.
5. Was intellectually challenging and rigorous (not to work much, but well); broke down resistance to new ideas; created an atmosphere that issues were serious and personal; daunting only such that students rose to the challenge; contended, struggled, encountered students (and any smugness of self-satisfactions), challenging and inspiring them to their best work; not readily satisfied, raised the bar; set higher (but with great effort) reachable standards.
6. Had, cultivated, and understood the worth of creating a (unique) teaching "personality"; created a "presence."
7. Had a sense of complete freedom from academic provincialism; had a mind characterized as having been washed clean of scholastic dust; had something of a quite jolly air of conscious insubordination, the mind impatiently dismissing the solemn snobbery of all that is academically canonized and sacrosanct.
8. Exhibited a certain insubordination, which occurs because of the great teachers' commitment to doing what works instead of what is conventional.

Characteristics of Great Teachers' Relationships with Their Students

9. Limited the insulation between the teacher and student in some meaningful way.
10. Always had one eye on the classroom, the other forever on the community; gave students a sense of what was going on "outside."
11. Maintained a certain relationship with students, not affection, but probably a respect that had a personal element.
12. Sought to impact each and every student in the class.
13. Had a certain kind of knowledge of individual students; knew which buttons to press to inculcate student growth.

Great Teachers' Effects on Their Students

14. Awakened, aroused, startled the student into thought. Made students think independently, stimulated independence of investigation by questions and suggestions; gave high importance to establishing habits of self-reliance; encouraged an exchange of ideas; made students ask and answer questions; sowed the seeds of students' intellectual and imaginative life; initiated inquiry; developed intellectual curiosity. Perhaps created a special class or program for advancing such aims.
15. Generated "contagious enthusiasm" among the students, creating an environment of a larger knowledge and a firmer purpose. The world seems bigger because of such teaching. The students in the class have a sense of being a learning community.
16. Carried students beyond the subject's boundaries; created an atmosphere of learning for learning's sake; had a formative influence on students' educational identities.

Aristotle (2002:30) argues, "But it is necessary not just to speak of this universally, but also to apply it to the particulars." This emphasis on applying ideas to particular examples suggests this study's approach: develop a working definition for "great teachers" and test it against the examples of thirty-two teachers who seem to be great individually. Thus, what is the relationship of the generalization to the particular?

This study posits that these thirty-two teachers, thought to be great teachers, do consistently exemplify these sixteen characteristics of great teachers. The immediate task of this study now becomes to match specifically these characteristics with these teachers thought to be great. What do these generalizations look like in the specific?

COMMENTARY ON THE CHARACTERISTICS

1. Had no fear of feeling and did not attempt to achieve that specious academic objectivity that can freeze a class.

    As observed in *Masters: Portraits of Great Teachers* (Epstein, 1981:31) about a great teacher, "When he became aware that any of the students he came to know were in trouble or distress his manner was gentle and kind." While the great teacher will tell the truth, more gently than the student may realize, about academic demands and academic performance, the great teacher does not presume to be the gatekeeper of academic excellence, but rather the source of knowledge and support to help the student make the necessary adjustments to achieve excellence. It is not about the objective knowledge but about caring enough for the student to help the student succeed.

2. Had thorough knowledge of the subject, whether that means by scholarship or by personal research; an original and penetrating intelligence; played easily with facts and ideas.

    As Rafe Esquith (2003:20) wonders in *There Are No Short Cuts*, "What happened to pursuit?" His question reveals both his confidence in his own basic academic knowledge such that he is quite comfortable exploring questions to which he does not have a ready answer and his emphasis on helping students engage in the pursuit of knowledge, more than simply learning and regurgitating some body of facts.

3. Had a rich fund of example, metaphor, and story to make the complex more simple and to make learning meaningful.

    As also mentioned elsewhere, Jim Herndon (1971) demonstrates this teacher quality in his writing. Even his student, Tizzo, agrees that no one should disturb the salamander in the terrarium, while nonetheless meddling with the creature. Herndon explains that schools are more about sorting and selection than education by likening it to sorting the sheep and the goats. He likens educators continuing to pursue ideas that do not work with Columbus failing to follow the gold-laden canoes to Incan destinations. He tells of the dog who would not give the ball up so that it could be thrown in a game of fetch to the teachers who will not give up certain practices so that learning can go on.

4. Was the "best" teacher, not necessarily the most "finished" teacher, often working through ideas struggling for expression, rather than simply presenting preformulated ones; exhibited an original and penetrating intelligence at work, playing freely with facts and ideas.

    Edmund Wilson (in Epstein, 1981:4) says about his teacher, Christian Gauss, "His own ideas on any subject were always taking new turns: the light in which he saw it would be shifted, it would range itself in some new context." Great teachers tend to be more spontaneous than finished. While they will have deeply considered the ideas that they are sharing, the ideas are reconsidered in ways such that they do not become trite for having been overly rehearsed. By emphasizing the constant process of discovery, they communicate vitality to students.

Wislawa Szymborska (1996) observes that "there is a certain group of people whom inspiration visits . . . their work becomes one continuous adventure as long as they manage to keep discovering new challenges in it. Difficulties and setbacks never quell their curiosity. A swarm of new questions emerges from every problem they solve. Whatever inspiration is, it's born from a continuous 'I don't know.'" Great teachers emphasize academic curiosity more than their own academic expertise. A teacher's expertise might suppress student interest, while a teacher's sense of inquiry more likely inspires.

5. Was intellectually challenging and rigorous (not to work much, but well); broke down resistance to new ideas; created an atmosphere that issues were serious and personal; daunting only such that students rose to the challenge; contended, struggled, encountered students (and any smugness of self-satisfactions), challenging and inspiring them to their best work; not readily satisfied, raised the bar; set higher (but with great effort) reachable standards.

In *Escalante: The Best Teacher in America*, Jay Mathews (1988:5) observes about the teaching of Jaime Escalante that students "can achieve results they never dreamed of. All they need is the drive and impatience and love that push a school and its students far beyond their assumed limits." All great teachers do this, but perhaps none better than Escalante in having Garfield High School calculus students compete and outdo the most privileged private school students in America on the national Calculus Advanced Placement Exam.

6. Had, cultivated, and understood the worth of creating a (unique) teaching "personality"; created a "presence."

George Brockway (in Epstein, 1981:156) also observed this characteristic of "presence" in his portrait of his teacher, Joseph Epstein. Each of the thirty-two teachers considered in this study created unique and memorable teaching personas. Each had that presence that helped their teaching, and while the intent was improving student performance, each presence also made them memorable, made them stand out. They had a gravitas, whatever else might be said about their personalities that immediately captured student interest and announced that they were to be taken seriously.

Such great teachers have star power, which is why they can be great from the beginning of their careers while still on the way to becoming expert teachers. Think of actors or actresses who obviously had star power in their first significant cinematic roles.

Tom Cruise in *Risky Business*, Julia Roberts in *Mystic Pizza*. Did they get better at their acting crafts? Undoubtedly, but they had the right stuff from the beginning.

The good news, great news for great teachers—the kind of charisma that a Cruise or Roberts has is not necessary for great teachers. Great teachers have something special, something that they find within themselves and develop. Great teachers dig deep inside, commit to being special for their students, doggedly push students to excel, and they develop a sensitive homeostatic device that alerts them to continue experimenting to find what works best for their students. At the end of the day, course, or career, great teachers are often remembered fondly, even by students with whom the teachers think that they may have failed, because those students may very well remember that whatever the results of that year of their lives, they had a teacher who did not quit on them.

7. Had a sense of complete freedom from academic provincialism; had a mind characterized as having been washed clean of scholastic dust; had something of a quite jolly air of conscious insubordination, the mind impatiently dismissing the solemn snobbery of all that is academically canonized and sacrosanct.

George Brockway (in Epstein, 1981:159), in discussing his great teacher, John William Miller, observes that "the courses varied from year to year, partly because they were to some degree shaped by the problems brought by the students." That the courses differed from year to year offers evidence of this lack of academic provincialism.

For the great teachers the courses must be different from year to year, because even if the foundations of the academic discipline have failed notably to change during the time between teaching the courses, the students are never the same. The freedom from academic staleness not only represents the open-ended possibilities of the subject but also the necessity to match the course content in the best way possible to the particular group of students.

8. Exhibited a certain insubordination, which occurs because of the great teachers' commitment to doing what works instead of what is conventional.

Great teacher Rafe Esquith (2003:2) admits, "I've never been one of the masses." Peter Stern and Jean Yarbrough (in Epstein, 1981:189–90) observe about great teacher, Hannah Arendt, that "she seemed to violate many of the canons that made for effective teaching," and they suggest that she could get away with this because of "the mysterious force of her personality."

Great teachers are walking challenges to the status quo. It is a large part of why so many others, especially lesser teachers and bureaucratic administrators, often resent them. There was an observation about legendary Georgetown basketball coach John Thompson, that went something like, "Mere normal folk wondered where and how he got so sure." Such a perception about great teachers (and undoubtedly about Thompson) tends to be misleading. Great teachers only tend to speak out on issues and ideas for which they have given much thought and study.

Great teachers are not the persons Will Rogers had in mind when he quipped that there was never a greater fool than the experts speaking outside their field. Somehow many reputed experts assume that they have authoritative knowledge in anything that comes to their attention. Great teachers tend to know that more is unknown than known. But since they also tend to have the courage to speak out in circumstances where they are pretty sure of something, and otherwise tend to pay attention and listen, they may be thought by some as arrogant rather than humble, because what is in public view and memory are the moments of forthrightness, not silence.

Meanwhile great teachers, knowing how difficult it is to tailor teaching to individual classes and individual students, continue to irk bureaucratic administrators who seek consistency, compliance, uniformity, and efficiency, as if there was one best way and that everyone should get with the program (regardless of whether the program is unproven, never worked, or has dubitable prospects of working with these students). By doing what is needed instead of expected, these great teachers are a pain. But they are necessary.

9. Limited the insulation between the teacher and student in some meaningful way.

Great teachers limit the insulation between student and teacher in ways unique to their individual approaches to teaching. Great teachers can seem imposing, but because they value a comparable independence of thought, as George Brockway (in Epstein, 1981:158) said about his teacher, John William Miller, "Agreement was not compelled, but understanding was required." Not only do all great teachers do this in their own way, they also do it differently student by student. As Brockway also observed about Miller (Epstein, 1981:160), "Finally, none of us knew more than a part of him—because there were so many of us . . . meeting each student on his own ground, he had many grounds to cover."

Often the limited insulation shows up as the great teachers become advocates for their students. In *Escalante: The Best Teacher in America* (Mathews, 1988:178), Jaime Escalante forthrightly responded to the challenges that his students had cheated on the Advanced Placement Calculus Exam, "I stand behind my kids." As Jay Mathews (1988:201) observed about Escalante's great teaching, "It makes the teacher the ally of the student against this outside force." This kind of protective and supportive attitude toward students also evidences itself in the teachers' writing of untold numbers of personal letters of recommendation.

Limiting the insulation permits the great teachers to read the individual students, the cliques, the roles, the class. Perhaps some great teachers are gifted in terms of Gardner's sense of interpersonal intelligence, but the critical difference between teachers who do and do not read a class well more likely lies in a willingness to do the reading of the class in the first place. Such teachers consistently recognize the lapses and failures with a class. The evidence? A student's frown may be unhappiness, or seriousness of intent. Which is it?

The use of seat work and small-group work affords the teachers the time and opportunity to connect with individuals and groups. Many or most students affect different personalities in different settings such as one-on-one, small groups, and the full class. Consistencies and inconsistencies in students' behavior, body language, and verbal comments and their interactions with other students offer clues about the needs, interests, and propensities of the students and can help the teacher match the lesson to the students.

Great teachers learn to recognize surprises and then are quick to find out from students what the surprises mean. The demands for rapport differ with individuals, cliques, and classes, but they rely upon mutual respect. By having a relationship founded upon respect, students can and will rise to meet the great teacher's loftier expectations.

10. Always had one eye on the classroom, the other forever on the community; gave students a sense of what was going on "outside."

Great teachers enlarge students' perspectives on the wider community and do so in unique ways consistent with their personalities and presumably in ways consistent with their own worldviews. Rafe Esquith in *There Are No Short Cuts* (2003:149) says, "When all is said and done, a good teacher helps the student to improve the quality of his (the student's) life." For those students sufficiently interested, Alice Coleman and John M. Daly made an Ivy League education possible and accessible. Coleman also personified a life enriched by the aesthetics of literature; Daly led students to be interested in current politics.

Pepperdine University history professor and university president, Howard White, observed that he did not know why athletics were so important to a culture, but they had been so throughout history. Coach Beck communicated to his students this indispensability of sports. Different in the particulars, the great teachers consistently place what they do with students in a larger perspective and context that promises to make students' lives richer and more meaningful.

11. Maintained a certain relationship with students, not affection, but probably a respect that had a personal element.

Great teachers simultaneously teach a class as an entity, influencing the class to impose its own standards and expectations of excellence, but also teach each student individually. All students are given the same opportunities but are not treated the same. Some students respond well to encouragement, others to the swift kick to the behind (metaphorically speaking, of course). Great teachers commit themselves to the long-term best interests of the student; some students will be headed toward Harvard, others toward parenthood, which will have its own separate demands for instilling purposeful lives in their own children.

In ways even the best parents cannot, great teachers can challenge students to exceed their current expectations. As Jay Mathews (1988:5) observes in *Escalante: The Best Teacher in America*, Jaime Escalante demonstrates that students "can achieve results they never dreamed of. All they need is the drive and impatience and love that push a school and its students far beyond their assumed limits." Great teachers know this to be true, and this becomes the most exhausting aspect of great teaching: convincing the students. The huge engines that move trains are not needed to keep a train moving but are absolutely necessary to get it moving and up to full speed.

Students both appreciate and resent this teacher recognition of their truer possibilities—honored by the recognition, but frustrated by the time and energy it will take them to invest in such positive changes. Great teachers find their payoffs, but it is not in the day-to-day "love" of their students, who mostly try to resist the teacher's efforts in heroic ways and only acknowledge their appreciation of the teacher's efforts in retrospect.

12. Sought to impact each and every student in the class.

Great teachers are talent scouts, so one of the reasons they teach each and every student is that they know they will discover some unpolished gems. Great teachers also know that the entire class can best drive an excellent student to the highest levels of success. Great teachers know that greatness in society has come from people who may have finished anywhere in the top to the bottom in a graduating class.

Great teachers know that students are looking to find what they need, and often take from a teacher something the teacher was at best dimly aware of having provided. Great teachers know that each and every student has talent and value that has an equal claim to being developed to its utmost. Great teachers know that the most successful students often needed the least from them. Great teachers value the equality of rights to life, liberty, and the pursuit of happiness.

13. Had a certain kind of knowledge of individual students; knew which buttons to press to inculcate student growth.

In *Escalante: The Best Teacher in America,* Jay Mathews (1988:42) found that it was Jaime Escalante's Bolivian mentor who first made Escalante aware that "a teacher has to be up on every trick . . . If it works, use it." The key to "if it works" is whether it will work with a particular student or students. The only way to make an educated guess about whether a ploy might work is to have good knowledge of the individual students so as to know what to try, and possibly in what order.

Such knowledge of students includes a willingness to let students assume leadership roles. Great teachers do not try to do too much work for the students, rather to encourage students to figure out the expectations and share those insights with other students. For example, in an Advanced Placement English class at Palisades High School, it became apparent that some of the students did not have the reading skills necessary to succeed. On their own initiative and not at the instigation of the teacher, some of the better students took it upon themselves to record the assigned readings so that other students would have the advantage of the read-along format to help them with comprehension. This student initiative and problem solving surpassed any advice the teacher might have given.

14. Awakened, aroused, startled the student into thought. Made students think independently, stimulated independence of investigation by questions and suggestions; gave high importance to establishing habits of self-reliance; encouraged an exchange of ideas; made students ask and answer questions; sowed the seeds of students' intellectual and imaginative life; initiated inquiry; developed intellectual curiosity. Perhaps created a special class or program for advancing such aims.

Elizabeth Cohen kept pressing her class of doctoral students. "You clarified the first and second norms, clarify the third and fourth." Her students tried, faltered, tried again, faltered, failed, only to be prodded with less and less patience by Professor Cohen. Finally she squinted, drew herself back slightly as if collecting herself, and then plunged the epee home. "You are Stanford doctoral students, yet you are unable to say that the second two norms about which this esteemed Harvard Sociologist has written are vague and overlap? Shame on you." Hers was a lesson far, far more valuable than only "learning" the meanings of the norms: achievement, independence, specificity, and universalism.

Leo Tolstoy (1967:309) in his *On Education* concludes that "it is necessary that he (the student) should like learning." This is integral to arousing thoughtful responses in students. In *Escalante: The Best Teacher in America*, Jay Mathews (1988:83) found that students "relished a challenge, if it was properly proposed." Certainly great teachers have the capacity to awaken student interests, but great teachers realize that it is their subsequent independence of thought that truly excites students.

15. Generated "contagious enthusiasm" among the students, creating an environment of a larger knowledge and a firmer purpose. The world seems bigger because of such teaching. The students in the class have a sense of being a learning community.

Perhaps the most dramatic public example of this contagious enthusiasm that leads to a sense of being in a learning community was Jaime Escalante's work with the Garfield High School students who successfully passed the Advanced Placement Calculus exam, were accused of cheating on that exam, and then again passed the exam on a second sitting. Most of the time great teachers' ability to create such enthusiasm and a sense of community are not covered by the national media, but the case of Garfield High School reveals what is endemic to great teachers' classrooms.

16. Carried students beyond the subject's boundaries; created an atmosphere of learning for learning's sake; had a formative influence on students' educational identities.

Because of the complexity and extent of human learning and understanding, surely no single course could in and of itself provide enough content to make an education. But great teachers find a way to make the particular class they are teaching a fulcrum to leverage curiosity into a lifelong pursuit. In *Masters: Portraits of Great Teachers*, Anthony Hecht (in Epstein, 1981:187) wrote about his teacher, John Crowe Ransom, "For one learned from him, not facts or positions, but a posture of the mind and spirit." That posture of the mind helps students transcend the particulars of the course subject. And that learning always takes place with great teachers in the context of a relationship with that teacher.

As Mayeroff (in Richardson, 2001:101) finds, "To care for another person, in the most significant sense, is to help him grow and actualize himself." Great teachers use the course curriculum to generate a commitment to learning, which in turn helps that student grow.

GREAT TEACHER STANDOUTS IN EACH OF THE CHARACTERISTICS

Being a great teacher is not a contest. As former Pepperdine University president, Norvel Young, liked to point out: "There is no competition among lighthouses." Nonetheless, best lists are fun to make and may help further clarify what makes great teachers different, even from each other. Thus work through the characteristics of great teachers, considering from our candidates who might be considered best and who the least suggests the range among great teachers, but they are not prescriptions, and the exploration may reveal some limitations about the characteristics. Here is the listing of the thirty-two Great Teachers used to consider the ins and outs of each presumed great teacher characteristic:

1. Gene Bream
2. Pete Dixon
3. Charlie Chang Park
4. Larry Giacomino
5. John M. Daly
6. Alice Coleman
7. Paul Beck
8. Lewis Owen
9. Royce Clark
10. Frank Hawkinshire
11. Fannie Shaftel
12. Elizabeth Cohen
13. Arturo Pacheco
14. Elizabeth Traugott
15. David Tyack
16. Elliot Eisner
17. Jim Herndon
18. Paulo Freire
19. Leo Tolstoy
20. Socrates
21. E. R. Braithwaite
22. Rafe Esquith

23. Gloria Ladson-Billings
24. Robert Inchausti's Brother Blake
25. Sylvia Ashton-Warner
26. Dave Levin
27. Mike Feinberg
28. Harriet Ball
29. Jaime Escalante
30. Ben Jimenez
31. Frank Corcoran
32. Joe Cattarin

1. No fear of feeling. Rafe Esquith shared such feeling with his students that he found it sometimes interfered with his success and he sometimes had to back off on his emotional commitment to students lest they feel overly obliged to him. Lewis Owen's feeling may have stemmed more from a passion for aesthetics than a less complex sharing of feeling. Fannie Shaftel seemed to have neither excess nor deficiency in sharing affect with her students, and she was unique in the way she created collegiate respectability for using role-playing for students to explore social values.
2. Keen intelligence. David Tyack may have been the most preeminent in knowledge of his subject, history of education. Elliot Eisner may have been the most erudite. Presumably Sylvia Ashton-Warner was required to have the least knowledge of any subject matter because her work was with preschool children, but she defined *teacher research* as she developed key vocabulary with Maori children.
3. Rich use of language. Elliot Eisner could bring examples from painting, opera, music, and theatre and from aesthetics, anthropology, and education. Jim Herndon could find the story that told the educational point in dogs who would not give up the ball to play catch, Christopher Columbus failing to notice the Incan canoes carrying gold, and how schools separate the sheep and the goats. John Daly spent less time needing to explain the history and more time on helping students learn to write academic arguments, and he would have profited from Joe Cattarin's great ability to tell his historical stories.
4. Thinks on her/his feet. With the probable exception of Socrates, Elliot Eisner was the most exciting from the list of great teachers to hear him think on his feet. He seemed to discover, but was presumably rediscovering, every idea that he discussed with a class. Lewis Owen was a great teacher despite his polish. One of many guest lecturers in Occidental College's two-year program in the History of Civilization, his lecture following a class essay exam not only answered that question comprehensively but also was so polished as to be envied by all the

undergraduates. Both Eisner and Owen were brilliant, but the edge
here favors the dynamic and improvisational qualities even over the
"finished" in regard to this characteristic of greatness.

5. Challenging. Socrates and Tolstoy are two of the most intellectually
   challenging teachers in history. From the more mortal on our list,
   Elliot Eisner was the most intellectually challenging and was as happy
   discussing Socrates, the polyfocal conspectus, thick description, and
   Andy Warhol. Coach Paul Beck was challenging, but not in the intellectual way associated with great teaching, which suggests that this
   great teacher characteristic might be better described using Gardner's
   eight intelligences (see chapter 4), and that a great teacher will be
   challenging in terms of the intelligence suggested by the subject itself,
   or even better as challenging as many kinds of intelligence as possible.

6. Unique teacher persona. As portrayed by Edward James Olmos, Jaime
   Escalante had perhaps the quirkiest persona among the core group of
   great teachers. Frank Hawkinshire was the most imposing character.
   David Tyack and Fannie Shaftel might have seemed too normal except that they had so conspicuously taken their great character, intelligence, and goodness to an obviously elevated level. The thirty-two all
   had memorable personas.

7. Sense of freedom. Elliot Eisner developed "educational criticism" as
   an alternative to mainstream quantitative research, and despite his
   ideas flying in the face of dominant expectations, he was elected the
   president of the American Educational Research Association. He was
   not only free of academic provincialism, he has been perhaps America's greatest recent challenger to it within the field of professional
   education. John M. Daly was politically a reactionary. He supported
   Barry Goldwater for president in 1964. More than any other of these
   great teachers he insisted on things being done his way. There is little
   doubt that Daly's conclusions stemmed from his own independent
   thinking, and if he preferred the traditional, it was not because it was
   provincial. Academic provincialism was anathema to one and all.

8. A certain insubordination. All these great teachers found their individual ways to get things done in their own way. Paulo Freire was run out
   of two countries for his success with literacy, so perhaps he was the
   most insubordinate, but then again, he did not refuse to leave and thus
   was able to write his books from some place other than jail. Perhaps
   Fannie Shaftel seemed the least insubordinate, but, reader, realize the
   significance that she found a way to get academic recognition for her
   creative work with role-playing.

9. Connects with students. Rafe Esquith and Jaime Escalante spent copious amounts of time with students year round, spent the most time
   eating with students, and spent the most time with their students'

families. Esquith regularly travels with his students. In terms of greater insulation Royce Clark used such "extra" time to start his own vineyard. This is not a criticism of Clark. What the great teachers have in common is limiting the insulation between students and teacher to what the students need. Esquith and Escalante simply had to have a closer personal relationship with their students than professors with most college students. All thirty-two easily made personal connections with students and enjoyed excellent rapport with them.

10. Lends wider perspective. Arturo Pacheco's concern for cultural pluralism was one of the most encompassing views of education that looked beyond the classroom at the greater community. All of these great teachers had significant sensibilities about "justice"—in the classroom, the school, the community, and society. From this list of great teachers the two who may have limited their teaching the most to their respective disciplines would be Coach Paul Beck and Professor Lewis Owen. This observation says more about the boundaries associated with these two subject matters than the great teachers themselves.

11. Relates to students. Hawkinshire was the scariest; Eisner was known to read his correspondence while meeting with students during office hours. Clark may have been invited to the most weddings. In their own individual ways, whatever else the character of their relationships, with students they were founded in great respect by the students for the teacher.

12. Dedicated to each and every student. Escalante probably fought the hardest to keep each and every student. Ben Jimenez might accept that a handful of students just were not well matched with Advanced Placement Calculus and let them transfer. No teacher who fails to try to reach every student makes the cut here as a great teacher.

13. Tailors teaching strategies to individual students. Escalante was a master at motivating students, figuring out how to challenge them. Shaftel assumed students would participate, and even ordinarily quiet students simply did so. While it may seem that some great teachers lead by example and some by using all the tricks of the trade, they all find and use what works best for them for maximum results.

14. Awakens students. Elliot Eisner encouraged his students to look for what is most neglected in their "educational criticism" of schools. Each of these great teachers filled a void. Gene Bream realized how pivotal junior high school can be; the KIPP teachers realized that many inner-city school students need a longer academic day, week, and year. John Daly and Alice Coleman created a combined Advanced Placement and Honors Program including English and history so that the cumulative effect would be greater. Rafe Esquith created the Ho-

bartian Shakespeare Company. Paulo Freire, a pedagogy for the oppressed. Those teachers also wrote books and reeducated perception.
All of these teachers aroused student interest, involvement, and action.

As suggested above in #5, this characteristic might be better framed
as challenging the kind of intelligence suggested by the specific kind
of subject, thus the physical-body connection for PE and Coach Paul
Beck, but this is not the only way Beck challenged. The Greeks had an
idea that competition was a means of improving individual performance, not a matter of winning or losing. Students respected Beck
because he so consistently challenged students to be better people, and
he happened to do this in the context of physical education and coach-
ing team sports. The great teachers arouse students to raise the bar of
their expectations.

15. Generates contagious enthusiasm. Students clamored to take courses
from these great teachers. Escalante accepted as many as fifty students
in a room that would not hold that many people. While Fannie Shaftel
had good enrollments, her students had to make something of a choice
to elect to take her courses. For all the idealism of learning for learning's sake, that was very much a part of the Stanford ethos, and as
much as role-playing for social values and studying with Shaftel
promised to make the student a better person, hers was not an area of
study that invited prestigious research or a dissertation.

As the great teacher candidate deliberates about what voids most
need to be filled among her/his teaching opportunities, the clout a new
intervention is likely to have has a political dimension that cannot be
ignored in making students' worldviews bigger and more encompassing.

16. Expands learning. Certain subjects may be more likely to have a
formative influence on students than others, and the timing in a student's life has its own influence. Arturo Pacheco had greater influence
on those students opening up to cultural pluralism than on those who
had already committed themselves to such a direction. John M. Daly
was extremely influential as he worked in tandem to create great educational aspiration among students who had not previously had such
aspirations. Jim Herndon established the relationship between surviving teaching and surviving one's native land. All these great teachers
would not have had the same impact upon all their students because
students do not need the same things. In fact, the great teacher knows
that students tend to find what they need from the teacher, even when

such may not have been what the great teacher thought she or he was offering. Even, no, especially, for great teachers the process remains more art than science, and mostly mystery.

Thus the scorecard above finds that overall the great teachers tend to validate Peterson's definition of great teachers, and the definition sets these teachers apart from other teachers. The biggest concern about the characteristics as a whole is that the concern for challenging all the ways of being intelligent becomes more of a watchword for great teaching and great teachers. **Teachers who only do these things for their top students are jerks, not great teachers.**

THE EXTENT OF INFLUENCE

Great teachers necessarily reach a wide variety of students, but inevitably they do not reach all, and sometimes alternative teachers solve some of those problematic exceptions. Jaime Escalante had colleague Ben Jimenez. A noisy greatness backed by a calmer greatness. John M. Daly's "pomposity" worked for most of his students, but not for all. Fortunately there were other routes at his Mission Bay High School for the college bound. Even though Great Teachers may never reach absolutely all of their students, that may not even be true because the influence can reach so far into the future, and even the "failures" may well remember that teacher who cared.

Chapter Three

Great Teachers' Strategies and Practices

Chapter 2 establishes the characteristics of great teaching and demonstrates its utility for describing great teachers. But how did they get that way? And how might a teacher try to be one? John Dewey says that the purpose of criticism is the reeducation of perception. His sense of "criticism" entails insight, not merely being critical. The list of characteristics of great teachers from chapter 2 helps in understanding and recognizing what sets great teachers apart but does not delineate the behind-the-scenes, underlying realities of great teaching.

This third chapter considers how great teachers set high standards; how they develop their teaching persona; how they use the curriculum and hidden curriculum; how they use their classrooms as laboratories, constantly refining and changing their art and craft; and how they develop a class's sense of being a learning community. This chapter also speculates about the implicit personal philosophies that help such great teachers work toward something greater.

The two greatest influences on this study, beyond the examples of great teachers, were Houston Peterson's 1946 book, *Great Teachers*, and Jay Mathews's books on Jaime Escalante, *Escalante*, and the great KIPP teachers featured in *Work Hard. Be Nice*. It should probably be acknowledged that such books can also be quite annoying. An unheralded great teacher wrote how much she resents such examples as described by Mathews. Not the teachers per se, but the concomitant expectations that seem to come with accepting such great teachers as being exemplary. A highly dedicated teacher herself, she complained that the insinuation is that such examples make it seem that she should give up what little personal life remains for her.

In fact, Rafe Esquith (also cited in *Work Hard. Be Nice.*) acknowledges that the incredible amount of time and money that he spent early in his career was irresponsible and did not lead to great teaching. If Americans were to depend upon overzealousness for great teaching, virtually all students would have to go a lifetime without having had a great teacher. Research has shown that teachers spend about fifty-five hours a week during the school year on teaching. To have the energy for truly great teaching, most great teachers would be well advised to "stay alive at fifty-five." The truth of the matter— great teachers do what they have to do to be successful. A great teacher may find time better spent at a concert than laboring over a detailed lesson plan that is not coming together. A great teacher may need a nap more than another cup of coffee. A great teacher may need to ignore a student, for the moment, until a more propitious time.

Perhaps an essential point for most great teachers is praxis—that back and forth between thought and action. Insight into what a student most needs is often found by the subconscious, which picks places like the shower, the grocery store, and the track to reveal what needs to be tried. Great teachers find their own rhythms and do not need to feel guilty about spending less time and personal money than a Jaime Escalante or Rafe Esquith.

Despite what he says about himself, Rafe Esquith (*Teach Like Your Hair's on Fire*) was a great teacher from the beginning, even if, perhaps, before his teaching was actually great. Morris Cohen (in Epstein, 1981:24) in writing about his own great teacher, Sidney Hook, asked, "What makes a great teacher?" Cohen's answer includes:"When we look back on our schooling, we remember teachers rather than courses—we remember their manner and method, their enthusiasm, and intellectual excitement, and their capacity to arouse delight in, or curiosity about the subject taught." Beginning teachers can evidence these qualities.

Even as a novice great teacher Rafe Esquith evidenced greatness in his enthusiasm, openness, commitment, integrity, and willingness to learn from experience. Was he satisfied with his early results? No. Is he satisfied with his current results? No. By his own testimony, he is just more satisfied than he was with his first twenty years of teaching. The evidence from Esquith's books on teaching substantiates very clearly that his strengths were also his weaknesses. For example, his sense of duty was at times a compulsive commitment that first led to his own poor health and near personal bankruptcy. But also, gradually and eventually, it led to becoming a great teacher for an extremely diverse student population. Esquith inspired great teaching in others, as documented in Jay Mathews's book, *Work Hard. Be Nice*. Mike Feinberg and Dave Levin borrowed and adapted (as stated elsewhere, great teachers gladly "steal" anything that works) Esquith's slogan for their students to be nice and work hard as they created the now national KIPP

(Knowledge Is Power Program) schools. Despite their own difficulties at the beginning of their teaching careers, Feinberg and Levin, for all their apparent early failure, also began their careers as great teachers.

What do burgeoning great teachers do differently than good, fair, and poor teachers? Mathews, who also wrote a book on yet another great teacher, Jaime Escalante, has identified many of the personal characteristics and developing habits of the great ones. Mathews establishes identifiable ways that great teachers accomplish great teaching. His work suggests and tends to substantiate this study's conclusion that great teachers set high standards, develop a great teacher persona, animate the curriculum and teach responsibility, use the class as a laboratory, and create a sense of community. Starting with the high standards . . .

SET HIGH STANDARDS

The lesson: "demand more than they think they have to give." (Escalante in Mathews, 1988:288)

Great teachers set high, and if seemingly unreachable at first, reachable expectations, and they challenge students to excel. Within that framework the emphasis may seem to be on the class's front-running students, but great teachers value the honest progress of all students, whatever level of achievement that may be.

A line from the film *The Paper Chase* suggests that nature of the challenge. Two law students see that Professor Kingsfield is in his classroom long before students are to arrive. The Timothy Bottoms character whispers to the other student, "We are going to have to get up very early to keep up with him." When great professors seem to be working harder than the students on behalf of the students, convinced that the students have more potential than they themselves are wont to admit, the Siren song is sung—the call becomes irresistible at first for some and then for other students.

The student peer group then becomes an ally in establishing the validity of such high expectations. After all, what student wants to disagree with the thought that they really do have more potential than they are currently realizing? Students themselves accept then promote a strong work ethic, realize that the course and teacher are important, and know that the "collective we" are serious.

One of the reasons it is so difficult to study the already recognized great teachers is that what they did to become so successful happened years earlier and their great teaching takes on a kinetic life not entirely dependent upon the here and now. This continuity in years of student expectations helps account for the necessity of great teachers to have a place, time, and program that allows them to realize great teaching.

As professional baseball players rise to higher levels in the minor leagues toward playing in the major leagues, coaches tell them, "What got you here, won't keep you here." Presumably higher levels of play demand even greater skill and higher performance to stay. Great teachers challenge their students not to rest or even rely upon previous success but to elevate performance. On a student's first paper in Advanced Placement English Alice Coleman wrote, "You are in eleventh grade now." The message—what got you here will not keep you here. However friendly or daunting such a message may be, great teachers throw down the proverbial gauntlet, challenging students to newer heights.

DEVELOP A GREAT TEACHER PERSONA

> Successful classrooms are run by teachers who have an unshakable belief that the students can accomplish amazing things and who create the expectations that they will. My students perform Shakespeare because I believe they can, because they know that last year's class did, because I explain to them how they will do it and then show them. As soon as they master the first page, they begin to have confidence in themselves. They raise their own expectations. (Esquith, 2003:53)

Such great teachers as Rafe Esquith have a conviction that all students can improve, learn, and more so than others might expect and students might otherwise want to let on.

While great teachers are thought of as real, as authentic, as genuine, great teachers who have taught for very long know much of great teaching is also great acting. Great teachers can loom forebodingly over a miscreant student at the same time they are laughing inside at some student foible. Great teachers find patterns that promise success as evident by the commonly agreed-upon characteristics of great teaching identified in chapter 2.

Thus it behooves the great teachers to develop a persona that alerts students immediately that something special is about to happen. John Daly had his Ivy League ties and military haircut. Alice Coleman had her pearls. Lewis Owen wore his English tweeds and University of London mystique. Religion professor Royce Clark drove a Mercedes. Fannie Shaftel seemed as if she might have a magic wand and have been the fairy godmother who made Cinderella a princess.

Aristophanes might have written *Clouds* about Elliot Eisner instead of about Socrates. Eisner's little red Alfa Romeo sports car might have belied his otherworldly image except for the way that his driving seemed unbounded by any lines or lanes. Elizabeth Traugott was probably there at the creation discussing with God what was meant by Logos. Frank Hawkinshire seemed equally prepared to win a street fight or an intellectual argument. David Tyack rode his bike and brought his dog to school. Jaime Escalante challenged his students to handball games. Rafe Esquith literally taught one day with his hair on fire.

The great teacher would do well to find a style (even of dressing), a quirkiness, a persona, that is 1) close enough to the teacher's "real life" personality as to be sustainable; 2) different enough to be "unique" while recognizable enough to be understood by students; 3) recognizable enough to signal to students that something special is expected to happen.

Great teachers' personas are purposeful. Great teachers do not just challenge students; they engage students. A social psychologist observed that students' beliefs are only as strong as they have been tested. The depth of a student's education is only as deep as it has been plumbed. A superior wrestler helps a novice wrestler improve by exerting just the right amount of pressure to force the learner to improve. Too much pressure—discouragement and failure. Too little pressure—no progress. No pain, no gain.

Laying the course materials out there for the students to learn does not likely engage the student with the material. Students may go through the motions, and even pass exams, but that is not the stuff for great learning. The great teacher certainly "works the material," even more so "works" the students, but in an engaging fashion that makes learning meaningful and personal.

Philip Jackson says that teachers are either mimetic or transformative. Mimetic teaching has the sense of the transmission of known knowledge. Transformative teaching has the heuristic sense of inculcating transcendent values. Great teachers do both, but the emphasis is upon the transformative. Great teachers certainly teach their subjects, and do so exceedingly well. However, that subject matter becomes the key to educational aspiration, becoming a more enlightened person, a more responsible citizen, a better person.

The great teacher persona incorporates more than just classroom teaching. While great teachers may prosecute underachieving students, the teachers look out for the interests of students as if they are a defense attorney. While a student's guilt may be germane to outside proceedings, the defense attorney great teacher represents the best case possible for the offending student, treats any private counsel as privileged, gives sound advice, and directs the students to other necessary resources. This is true whether the student's situation demands a speech therapist, drug rehab, protection from domestic violence, or a stay from a suspension or expulsion.

A great teacher's private politics remain private. Is the student a child of an illegal alien or an undocumented worker? Regardless of the great teacher's personal politics, that student has a right to be in at least most states' public schools, and if that student sees himself or herself as the child of an undocumented worker, the teacher gives full respect to that student's point of view.

Whatever the uniqueness of the teaching persona, it communicates the teacher's decision to put students on notice that something special is expected to occur. Peter Stern and Jean Yarbrough (in Epstein, 1981:189–90) remark about their great teacher, Hannah Arendt: "She seemed to violate many of the canons that made for effective teaching," and they attributed much of her success to "the mysterious force of her personality."

These teachers develop an effective teaching persona, as varied as the teachers themselves, but that consistently captures the regard of their students. Deeply based in strong personal values, commitment, responsibility, and integrity. As Mathews says about KIPP teachers, "Their toughness (becomes) a part of their reputations." *Respect*, as a quality, works more convincingly and assuredly than popularity, and, ironically, ends up resulting in more popularity in the long term.

From such apparent toughness young great teachers practice "that voice, the combination of distress and love" for handling recalcitrant students. That voice does not happen automatically. Too much distress in the voice and the message to students is a lack of caring; too much love can be misread as a sign of weakness and low expectation. Great teachers manage to find that voice that communicates both distress and love simultaneously and clearly. Reasonably undaunted by their own weaknesses, great teachers recognize that "success depends as much on (their own) leadership as on the quality of the concept" that they work with.

In a sense this is a repetition of the idea that there are no teacher-proof curricular materials. For example, whether studying Gardner's eight intelligences or trying to appreciate them in a class of students, the key is not just the idea of eight intelligences so much as the leadership the teacher uses in making those ideas work with students.

> The difference between the best ones (teachers) and the others is that the best ones always get up to answer the bell. (Esquith, 2003:x)

Esquith also explains that great teachers become more aware of their own failings, thus the only way for a great teacher to prevail is to "answer the bell."

While being a great teacher presupposes great character, all those with great character do not become great teachers. While great teachers do not have "a" personality type, great teachers, even first-year great teachers, have an uncanny willingness to look their failures in the face and learn from them. A reason great teachers so often have unusual success with otherwise problem students is that these teachers have learned best of all that these students make them grow the most as teachers and as people. While great teachers know that teaching and learning is a two-way street, they look first at themselves for what else might have worked better with a student.

THE CURRICULUM AND HIDDEN CURRICULUM

Curriculum Vitality

Perhaps good teachers see themselves in a good job. Demanding, but only for 180 days a year. Perhaps excellent teachers see their subject matter as a great hobby, but as such only a special interest. Great teachers find their subject matter as the key to a good life. Escalante and Jimenez found that calculus could propel students into fulfilling futures; Levin, Feinberg, Bell, and Corcoran found that basic academic skills, doing well in school, could propel students to college and life success. Daly and Coleman valued Advanced Placement for what it did for promoting future lives of excellence, just possibly including an Ivy League school education. Owen found literature as the door to becoming cultured.

Clark found religion to be a study of life. Shaftel used role-playing to create social value. Hawkinshire reveled in a world of fascinating social dynamics. Traugott was midwife to the perceived world created by language. Tyack esteemed the perspective afforded by history. Eisner saw the world as a painter does, but that education could yield imagination and an enlightened eye. Pacheco opened the richness of cultural pluralism. Students sensed that these great teachers taught because in a sense they found teaching necessary to their identities and that what they taught was not only vital to how they approached the world but also had the same possibilities for their own students.

Organizing the Curriculum

Great teachers seem much more likely to rely on what John Dewey referred to as a psychological organization of the curriculum than a mechanistic one. Since research on student learning tends to show that students reorganize their learning according to what they previously knew, what might seem to be a logical organization if one were programming computers, may not work as well as the teacher presenting material only as the teacher recognizes that students are ready for such new knowledge, or organic teaching. The research also confirms that teacher overpreparation tends to lead to inauthentic teaching, the insisting upon the dictates of the lesson instead of the changing needs of the class.

Thus deliberately or intuitively great teachers create learning spaces in their curriculum. Perhaps the reading assignments are organized into a syllabus, but plenty of time is left within each classroom period, unit, and term to use time wisely, whether helping students anticipate what comes next, developing a reading skill necessary for the unit, and attending to classroom dynamics that help or hinder class progress.

Great teacher and author Jim Herndon raised the issue of "Noman." Noman represents that voice of the usual ways of doing things that warns reticent teachers against trying anything different. Two young, great teachers showed evident relief in the affirmation that they need not handcuff their teaching with the institutional expectations for seemingly minute-by-minute syllabi. They reported that they had been somehow reluctant to emphasize in their own teaching what consistently worked best, which was working the overall course material at the most teachable moments.

They were both also encouraged to be sure to remind their own students of the heuristic advantages of such psychological organization of the curriculum so that their students did not report them as being disorganized at their end-of-term student evaluations.

The Hidden Curriculum

Philip Jackson coined the term *the hidden curriculum*. This refers to the implicit lessons also taught during the conduct and context of any explicit, formal curriculum. Jackson found that the lessons of the hidden curriculum include *power*, *praise*, and *crowds*. That is, schools ordinarily teach students to accede to the teacher's power, work primarily for the teacher's praise, and to put up with being treated as a member of a group instead of more personally. Michael Apple emphasizes that schools teach *compliance* and *conformity*.

Great teachers resist teaching these common, implicit lessons of the hidden curriculum. While accepting the responsibilities of their own authority, these teachers emphasize the student's personal and independent responsibility, intrinsic satisfactions instead of external praise, their students being autonomous individuals and free thinkers. Such "values" as conformity and compliance sufficiently offend great teachers that such behavior is not so much discouraged as it is beneath the acknowledgment of great teachers who expect and give students full respect.

The great teacher might have recommended ways for students approaching that particular course's challenges but with no rigid prescriptions or hard-and-fast rules. Life and school are too ambiguous for such certitude. If students find a different approach that works, such effort is not "tolerated," it is celebrated, and it can become exemplary for future student efforts.

William Saroyan said something to the effect of: teachers teach but one course, themselves. Great teachers find how this course that they are teaching at this time might be the most important that a student might ever take. Prospective great teachers take note: make it so. Find the way your subject matter in this class that you are teaching was or might have been pivotal, the fulcrum of your own success, and communicate that honestly to students as to how this can be true for them.

USING THE CLASS AS A LABORATORY

The Classroom as a Place to Solve Problems

> Great teachers use their classrooms as labs. Oser recognizes this in discussing the implications of Piaget. She notes Piaget's statement—that teachers who convey only knowledge without considering the operations of students inhibit student learning—must be taken more seriously. . . . We must train teachers to pose and to test hypotheses about what students are doing cognitively and emotionally when teaching is going on. (Oser, in Richardson, 2001:1061)

Jay Mathews observes that great teachers see their classes as laboratories. They learn from experience. They have a "willingness to change, and quickly, when students don't improve."

Great teachers pose and test hypotheses as if their classrooms were where the teacher constantly experiments to find what works. This analogy tends to break down because what worked one day with one class with one student may fail the next day, with the same class and same student. In this regard the challenge may be more like that of a great late-night program host, adjusting moment by moment, making even the bad jokes work somehow to keep the kinetic energy flowing.

Another limitation of the lab analogy is the thought that science might reveal best practices. "Best practices" can cause more problems than they solve. While the so-called best practices may provide a good place for the teacher to start, that they worked for most students elsewhere does not guarantee that they will work with your particular group of students. The temptation very well may be, then, to blame the students for failing to respond to best practices and persist with what has been proven to work elsewhere, even when it does not work for these students.

Again, great teachers constantly adjust to find what works with these students this day, and this is why the lab analogy remains a useful one. Since not one of the teacher's students is likely, for example, to graduate with a degree in the teacher's subject, the teacher not only knows more than the student now knows about the subject but also likely more than they will ever know. So the process involves matching teachable moments with as much significant learning as possible. This requires constant experimentation; the class becomes a place to solve problems.

Finding Other Ways to Progress: Taking Risks

Great teachers take risks. Emphatically what worked for great teachers at one place and time might not even work for them elsewhere. But they go out of their way to try things they can think up that are not being done by others. John Daly "went on strike," refused to teach any longer until his class could convince him that they were going to work as necessary. Alice Coleman could give tongue-lashings like no other. Regardless of prohibitive rules against such, Daly made his college-bound students buy the college history text, T. A. Bailey's *The American Pageant*, and ignore the dutifully provided official course text.

Physical Education teacher Paul Beck had students chip in money that would only be used to buy treats for the members of the class's winning team. Daly ceremoniously tossed underperforming students from his class with no promise of readmission. The college professor, who locked his classroom door refusing to admit late students, might have made that practice work, except that he taught only to the top of his classes.

College dean and statistics professor Ben Culley visited students on Sunday evenings in their dorms. Culley also carried around a large wad of cash from which he lent students interest-free money for emergencies, taking only an IOU as collateral. Understood to be for emergencies, Culley seemed to take special delight one Sunday evening in visiting a sophomore, who had borrowed money from him for ostensibly pressing reasons, and asking the student if he might listen to the quality of the stereo that the student had just purchased with those emergency funds. Culley did not file a complaint or judgment against the student. In the kindest of demeanors Culley simply asked him about the woof of the speakers.

Elliot Eisner placed the titles of readings that students should read in his syllabus. He did not feel constrained to cover all of these works in class or on his exams. Eisner would permit students to submit "icons" other than term papers. Frank Hawkinshire and Fannie Shaftel included a student's own evaluation in the student's grade.

David Tyack expected even his nonhistorian students to complete an original study of documents and write a history. When a doctoral student confessed that he could not account for the unlikely changes purported in a school district's year-to-year report, Tyack just looked at the student, and then looked some more, and yet some more, and finally it occurred to the student that the purported institutional changes had not actually occurred, only that different pictures had been taken to make such changes appear to have happened.

Such out-of-the-ordinary practices suggest risk and unsure results and that great teachers were not working from someone else's list. Great teachers rely upon intuition to try such measures because they defy common expectations. Such tactics may work short term, long term, with some students and not others. But they make an impression, and because the great teacher's classroom is a lab, unique and unusual strategies can be experimented with and kept or left according to what further developing circumstances reveal.

Great teachers rarely apologize to classes because their efforts are so single-mindedly with the students' best interest at heart. But especially on an individual basis, and privately, great teachers can and do apologize if they truly caused a breach with a student.

Sometimes the experiments seem odd but work out in the long term. Great teachers take risks. Dartmouth-educated Peter Tracey simply sat at the front of his classroom on the very first day until students spoke up and asked questions—however long that might take. The first day, week, or month might elicit paucity of conversation, but by the end of the year the class is full of student-initiated inquiry.

The Commitment to Change

One of the finest accounts of a teacher's commitment to change can be found in Leo Tolstoy's account of his teaching at a village school in *On Education*. Tolstoy (1967:299) emphasizes: "I made mistakes." Tolstoy (227) had an acute awareness of how fluent teaching must be. He observes: "Like all living beings, the school not only becomes modified with every year, day, and hour, but also is subject to temporary crises, hardships, ailments, and evil moods."

No amount of planning can account for all the variables that will occur in any teaching moment. Thus Tolstoy (3) "considered it his duty to assist the children in their search for knowledge by adjusting his method of approach to the individual child." Even the accomplished literary giant found that when it came to teaching, he had to commit to daily adjustments and change.

The acclaimed teacher of Maori children, Sylvia Ashton-Warner, committed herself to discovering the changes that were obviously necessary when she moved from New Zealand to teaching in an American school. Ashton-Warner (1972:172) concluded that

> a style of teaching suiting one nation does not necessarily suit another. A look into schools, Asian and Western, is to see the subtle differences in children and the not always subtle differences. What my apprenticeship in our school is reminding me, as I've said before, is that children differ not only from country to country but from state to state; from city to city and from school to school. Nor is that all; from teacher to teacher and from child to child. Only the organic style, the material coming from the mind of our child himself, wherever he is, whatever color he is, can accommodate him. Only his own clothes fit him.

These truths commit great teachers to great changes as required class to class, student to student. Thus, inevitably the great teacher makes adjustments. In *Masters: Portraits of Great Teachers*, George Brockway (in Epstein, 1981:159) observes about his teacher, John William Miller, that "the courses varied from year to year, partly because they were to some degree shaped by the problems brought by the students." Great teachers do not have a one-size-fits-all curriculum, and whatever their subject matter, they are committed to matching the best of the subject with the actual students they have.

This is what E. R. Braithwaite found and was willing to do with his London students. In *To Sir, with Love*, Braithwaite (1959:66) had to admit, "But if I had made so little impression upon them, it must be my own fault, I decided it was up to me to find some way to get through to them. Thereafter I tried very hard to be a successful teacher with my class, but somehow, as day followed day in painful procession, I realized that I was not making the grade." So he committed himself to whatever change would be necessary (72). "(The) next morning I had an idea . . . (76) (I) felt more than ever determined to make a success of the class." This commitment to change by great teachers evidences why Jay Mathews concludes that great teachers treat their classrooms like laboratories, experimenting until they find what works.

Jim Herndon (1965:126) in *The Way It Spozed to Be* had a similar realization to Braithwaite's. What Herndon was doing was not working with his students. He writes that "after all the advice: I figured I was on my own . . . I wanted solidarity as a class for 7H and the figuring out of their own possibilities and desires for 9D . . . I'm trying to make it clear that I was concerned for them as they were, now, in my class. . . . After the visits and advice, I was able to get going, I stopped trying to 'figure out' methods that were foolproof or 'the best' . . . and I simply started in with everything it had occurred to me to try out." The failure is an aspect of great teaching as it becomes the spur to continue to experiment until something truly worthwhile does work.

This is also the story of Herbert Kohl (1967:192). Kohl says that "confronted by the human challenge of the classroom I reached into myself, uncovered a constant core which enabled me to live with my mistakes and hypocrisies, my weaknesses and pettiness; to accept myself as myself all the many contrary and contradictory things I was. I fought to be more human and feel I succeeded." Great teachers are at least as susceptible to failure as others, perhaps more so. Great teachers simply persevere, continue to stare failure in the face, until they arrive at something worthwhile.

Anecdotal evidence indicates that their students appreciated the very effort far earlier than the great teachers themselves did. Students are more likely to recognize and appreciate the commitment, while the great teachers remain focused on finding a self-imposed, elevated level of success.

The young teacher outlined what the course would entail. Scrapped the plans by that first Friday. The early evidence was that the plans had no chance of working with these students. The willingness to admit this and not to blame the students characterizes the budding great teacher.

Meanwhile, great teachers overteach the vitals, the essentials for success in that course's subject matter. For John M. Daly "R.T.P.—read the problem. Introduce, Support, Conclude." All important for writing academic arguments successfully, not only in his Advanced Placement History class but also in future college coursework. As great teachers pursue what will work with their students, they are constantly finding such "scaffolding" that helps students handle difficult material and new challenges. Great teachers are committed to their subject matter, but they are even more committed to finding the most important components for their particular students.

Delight in the Process

Such teachers feel that "there was nothing better than trying out something that might help kids learn." For these teachers, "the better course was to solve problems logically, even if no one else was doing it that way." Alas, the "no one else" suggests the great divide between the great teachers and all others. Perhaps only the great teachers "looked around for some other way to take their students to the next level."

Jay Mathews describes such principles as the key to the particular kind of success that KIPP schools have had in particular, especially urban inner-city school settings. "That commitment to change in response to bad results became a KIPP axiom . . . to take what worked . . . to toss out the rest . . . adjusting to a changing world and to new information to help children."

Beyond the commitment to learning from your experiences with your own students and to delight in the process, nothing done elsewhere may end up working with your own students, but studying others' success has the potential of expanding your knowledge of the possibilities.

Thus, emphatically, particulars in this book, and especially in this section, are not "teacher proof"—guaranteed to work, even for great teachers. They merely offer perspectives that may help problem solve what the momentary lapse in student learning requires to keep moving forward.

CREATE A LEARNING COMMUNITY

> They truly believe that Latino students can succeed in school . . . it requires a teacher to fight inertia and human sympathy. (Mathews, 1988:289)
> (Escalante's) own challenge was to invigorate his most listless and discouraged students. . . . he tried to pick fights with them over dress, or tardiness, or anything that might engage their anger, and then their interest. (Mathews, 1988:84)

"Your" students. Students of great teachers somehow remain their alumni for life. That sense of commonality in a great teacher's classroom is inculcated from the first moment of such a class, and that sense of legacy remains a primary reason for a great teacher to find a particular work place to preserve as long as possible that sense of heritage for students. The thought that alumni might be able to visit a favorite teacher lends a bit of stability and continuity to their sense of life.

High Expectations Can Cause Students to Turn to Each Other for Help

As emphasized elsewhere as well, the great teachers will be most recognized for having raised the bar of expectations. Very often the students' sense of community begins in quiet desperation, that only by aligning with other students will it seem like the student can survive this new challenge, ordeal, crucible that comes with this great teacher in this demanding class. Machiavelli argues that it is safer to be feared than loved, at least with some of the citizens. Especially after having established a very demanding reputation, the great teacher can accept that she or he may at times seem intimidating, and that this can work toward a long-term good (as long as the intimidation is not true).

After all, telling students the truth about the quality of their work, even when done so gently, may seem intimidating to students used to doing less than they are capable of doing. Should the students raising their own bar of expectation, aspiration, and accomplishment begin with an "us against the teacher" dynamic, moving students to help each other, this can be a very effective first step in establishing the class as a learning community. Jaime Escalante did this exceedingly well as he challenged, confronted, cajoled, and invested in his students. But he was always there for them.

Alice Coleman frightened her students, then gave them the opportunity to work together to manage their stress. She established high standards, assigned copious amounts of writing, spent the time to read that writing. Sometimes she would maximize results by having students write five essays and pick their best one. She would only grade that one, or she would look over the others and grade a different one if it promised the student a higher grade. That generosity and understanding helped with the stress. She would also break students into small groups and have them give each other feedback on each other's writing, helping them to clarify the standards and further improve their own writing and establishing expectations that students will work together in a learning community. In such classes great teachers establish that it is "absolutely unacceptable for one student to make fun of or laugh at another student."

In its brevity this point seems less encompassing than the others on the list for creating a sense of community. It is written in the negative, what students must not do. It is extremely specific for a major factor in developing community. Nonetheless, Mathews makes an astute point in this observation about what set the KIPP teachers apart from others. Great teachers tend to find that a group is only as strong as its weakest link. For anyone to become a scapegoat within a group disavows the reality that real community exists. One of the primary roles for a good teacher, and also for a great teacher, is to protect all the members of the group. The message that it is absolutely unacceptable for one student to make fun of another student clearly communicates the equality of rights of each and every member of a just community.

Common Purpose

Although more obvious in an elementary school classroom where children spend the full day, week, and year with each other, all great teachers, even the youngest, try to create the sense of common purpose that Mathews (2009, 178–79) describes: "We are a team and we are a family. Not only do we respect one another's differences, but we celebrate them. We live together, learn together, take care of one another, and have fun together . . . (our) credo (is) if there is a problem, we look for a solution, if there is a better way, we find it, if a teammate needs help, we give it. If we need help we ask." Experienced great teachers may create such an environment more expertly, but with the enthusiasm of youth (and being closer to the same age as the students), young great teachers often do this exceedingly well. This sense of community is encompassing of all the class's students. When they were young, great teachers, an experienced great teacher (Harriett Ball) showed Feinberg and Levin how to make sure that no student was ignored and how to find something in each lesson that meant something to each student. Whether such a goal is possible every day with every lesson is doubtful, but great teachers ensure this happens regularly for all students, changing things as necessary to ensure that it does.

Paul Beck was a great teacher who taught physical education. By high school senior year his students would have previously learned something about soccer, track, handball, sprints, relays, softball, cross country, basketball, and softball. Beck would also anticipate that second-semester seniors presumably had senioritis. Not in his classes. He created teams that had parity. Made each student chip in some cash to pay for treats for the members of the winning team. Set up his own Olympic contests, changing sports each day and keeping team win-loss rankings.

Senior athletes worked harder for this class than they had for their respective varsity sports. And as even the second-place finishers envied the winners, a warm glow radiated from all the students from the athletic fields by Mission Bay because the semester had been great. Especially because of the trash talk among competitors, that may or may not have been within Beck's earshot. Was that enigmatic look that he had so often a smile?

For any PE teachers reading this work, great teacher Monty Steadman added a wrinkle to the class-teams way of organizing physical education. The teams in his classes would compete in the same sport for perhaps three weeks. He would have an odd number of teams and work with the unscheduled team on fundamentals, rules, skills, and strategy. He also instituted a weekly draft in which the last-place team could draft someone from the first-place team to improve its chances of winning. (Two players could be protected on each team.) The next-to-last team would draft from the second-place team, and so on. This practice kept the competition more balanced and also caused students to have an awareness of all the members of the class, which contributed to their greater sense of community.

Steadman also found that students with iffy attendance or recalcitrant attitudes could jeopardize the class's success. So each period one of the PE teachers volunteered to supervise all of the problem students. This kept the energy level high on the team competitions and tended to influence the problem students to change their attitudes so that they could return to all the fun.

Monty learned none of these strategies in his credential program, a book on methods, or from any other coach. His classes were his lab, and this program evolved out of his trial-and-error approach to making PE a meaningful place for students and to giving them a sense of common purpose, of community.

Spending Class Time on Whatever Supports the Teaching of the Subject

Fortunately, somehow this approach to teaching also results in a class's improved performance on standardized tests. Perhaps because emotion and reason are so intimately related, because academic motivation tends to generalize, time spent on class issues removes barriers to long-term scholastic success. The KIPP schools, celebrated for raising their students' standardized scores, spend time on "life skills: how to behave in different situations, how to persevere, how to be kind, how to help others." Apparently such time is "time on task" because those same students, then, do better in their more obviously academic work. Great teachers spend the time on any variable that interferes with or improves the classroom as a learning environment.

Great teachers take every opportunity to support each student in nonclass ways that do make the learning community an actual community. A small group of students were listening to two teachers discuss movies. This conversation took place in the late 1960s, and great art teacher Henry Rubio oddly inserted into the conversation that Ali McGraw was his candidate for most beautiful actress. Why did he add that to the conversation?

Henry said that McGraw seemed the most beautiful to him because unlike the perfect image of most actresses, McGraw seemed to him real, because her teeth were a little crooked. Even in this informal chat about movies Henry was vigilant about building up students in every way possible, including in this case the very pretty student who might have otherwise been self-conscious about her front teeth. Henry's greatness was in the fullness of his concern for each and every student. Such concern creates trust that affirms community. Consequently like with Esquith, students learn about the subject and about life.

Community—Creating an Atmosphere of Appreciation, Trust, and Truth

> My mission statement was now complete. In addition to "There are no short-cuts," the class was now taught four additional words: "Be nice, work hard." (Esquith, 2003:100)
> I stand behind my kids . . . It makes the teacher the ally of the student against this outside force. (Jaime Escalante in Mathews, 1988:178, 201)

Three qualities that might summarize the atmosphere in great teachers' classrooms: appreciation, trust, truth. Truth sets the context for tough love. The great teacher earns the right to tell the truth to students who have the capacity and need to improve. Curiously the great teacher often assumes the role of

prosecuting attorney in class ("Are you satisfied with this?"), while being the
public defender outside of class ("This student is an asset in my class and
needs this").

Larry Giacomino and Nick Leon took students on countless backpacking
excursions. All of their students did not need to go on these trips for all of
their students to benefit, to feel that they were in a community of learners
where such things were done together. They sometimes included "ropes
courses" on their excursions that literally required students to trust each other
to get over certain terrain.

What kind of evidence indicates whether true community has been
achieved? One of the strongest indicators is whether the individual members
take personal and overt responsibility for preserving its well-being. If the
school's recreational areas happen to be unsupervised, do the students still
act responsibly? If someone violates an important school standard, do other
students sanction that person? If there is a student performance, whether a
musical, play, or sporting event, do students hold each other responsible for a
best effort?

Jim Herndon recounts that at the end of his first year of teaching, his were
the only students to ignore the school riot that was taking place and to
continue with their class work. Jay Mathews tells the story of a KIPP teacher
who was inadvertently very late getting back to class, only to find one of his
students had taken over its direction. A strong indication of a successful class
would be whether the class goes smoothly for a substitute teacher. Whatever
the subject matter, such learned lessons of responsibility to community are
the greater ones.

A Final Note about Protecting Community

In such regards the great teacher takes personal insult at any expression that
might insult a student. If someone makes a sexist remark, that remark should
offend everyone. If someone makes a racist remark, it should offend everyone. If someone slanders a religious group, it slanders everyone. A great
teacher does not have to be a member of that group to take something personally even when it is without regard to that great teacher's sex, ethnicity, or
religious beliefs. An epithet directed toward any student is an epithet taken
personally by the teacher.

The Larger Sense of Community

> Gradually I was acquiring a real understanding, not only of the youngsters in
> my charge but also of the neighborhood and its people. (Braithwaite,
> 1959:151)

Is great teaching easy? Obviously not; even merely good teaching is incredibly demanding. Is great teaching always successful? No. But neither does anyone have a clear idea of where its influence ends.

The demands of teaching are great, results unknown. But is great teaching beyond your capacity? It need not be. The better question—are you willing to pay the price? You will have great success, but somehow that does not make the failures any easier. No teacher is ever prepared for the amount of failure experienced on a daily basis. The great teachers cringe, realize that failure is more widespread than they would otherwise like to acknowledge, and resolve to try yet something else until they find something that works, because what worked with fourth period today just may not work with sixth period.

Thus while living in the moment, the sense of community expands over both space and time. The long-term commitment (mostly) prevails. You can be a great teacher your first year. You will come to realize that great teaching is a journey, a quest, not a destination, that the commitment will mean more to your students than even the expertise that you develop over the years.

Great teachers, then, make the students' world a larger place geographically and over time. Esquith's elementary students perform Shakespeare, travel even to other countries. Esquith's, Levin's, Escalante's, Jimenez's, and Corcoran's students learn that college is within their reach. Great teachers inspire their students to pursue culture, to be creative, to continue with their formal and informal education. Conversely, these cultured great teachers find their own world deepened and enriched by the particularity of the lives and backgrounds of their students. Continuity within both space and time.

Great teachers appreciate students in the here and now but also realize that students are en route to an unknown destination. Because of an expanded awareness of time, they call upon all of their experience of humanity to identify and point out a student's strengths, possible school or career directions, and contributions that the student makes to the success of a class, whether it is ballast or energy.

"COMMON" PRACTICES

Great teachers often start their very first class in the middle of what they expect their students to learn to do. Like a James Bond movie inevitably begins in the middle of an action sequence, the great teacher may begin the very first class in the middle of a problem solvable by that class's subject matter. Ordinary, boring, conventional teachers are the ones who introduce themselves, have students introduce themselves, go over the syllabus, if college, and let the class go early. The great teacher often runs the first class overtime, creating the first impression that the class is important, serious, and not to be taken lightly, and will spend all of its time wisely.

With regard to the syllabus, great teachers know that the shorter the syllabus the better. Research indicates that the longer the syllabus, the less likely the student is to read it. But the more important consideration for the great teacher is that the longer the syllabus the more difficult it will be to make adjustments and changes along the way and to be assured of having enough available, seemingly unscheduled teaching spaces to respond to the class's greatest needs and interests.

Presumably if a student truly understands a course objective, they have previously mastered that objective. So while great teachers may bow to administrative pressure to include some well-meaning written objectives but (with Joseph Schwab and Ralph Tyler) know that objectives are more complex and interrelated than usually written, they tend to represent only what is most easily written, neglect socialization issues a la the hidden curriculum, and tend to neglect important but more diffuse learning aims.

Great teachers do not hide behind a point system, so whether an 89.5 percent is a "B+" or an "A-" is not an issue. Great teachers look for a pattern of excellence for "A's" and some level of personal responsibility for the historical "gentleman's 'C.'" Great teachers do not grade on the basis of the MLA style sheet, and while the lesser assignments may help the lesser student's grades, the highest grades go to the truly best performances because eventually excellence matters most, and anything less along the way was only intended to be a part of the journey that helped or didn't help that student to progress.

Great teachers may or may not accept a late paper. After all, a cumulative final exam should be sufficient for the task of assigning a course grade. But the great teacher does not downgrade a late paper—it is hard enough already to give students accurate feedback about the actual quality of their work.

If it is a lecture class and/or all the requisite course material is available in the reading for a college class, attendance need not be expected or required. More likely the great teacher is also establishing a learning community, thus all members need to be committed to being there all of the time.

The great teacher respects the students' time, so establishing what might be a demanding but reasonable reading list at the beginning of a course seems prudent, as is the number of major assignments and dates of exams. But an astute great teacher will leave enough flexibility to renegotiate the "agreements" of a syllabus and to change dates and adjust assignments—not arbitrarily, but reasonably and by agreement. A great teacher just would not suddenly add a new book, paper, or exam out of the blue.

At least in classes under forty students, almost all great teachers learn their students' names. A sure sign of respect.

Great teachers do not require students to organize small study groups, but an indicator that the teacher and course have been made appropriately challenging is for small groups of students to form to ensure their own success. This is apparently a common practice for first-year law students, and it is an indicator of great teaching success at least as early in school years as high school.

Would Tom Cruise wear a name tag? Students will find out what they want to know about their teachers, so at least most great teachers probably do not feel the urge or need to say much about themselves personally, especially in the early days of a class. Like the teacher's greatest need for a successful class is the knowledge of her/his students, great teachers let students learn what they need to know about the teacher as their ongoing relationship develops. (P.S. In regard to the 89.5 percent cited above, any teacher who would for some reason have a student with a score of 89.5 percent and not round up to 90 percent and an "A" is not a great teacher, is not an excellent teacher, is not a good teacher, is not only a poor teacher, but also a failure in life.)

THE GUIDING LIGHTS?

What are the guiding lights for great teachers?

> In bringing up, educating, developing, or in any way you please influencing the child we ought to have and unconsciously do have one aim in view,—to attain the greatest harmony possible in the sense of truth, beauty, and goodness. (Tolstoy, 1967:220)

By their venerable examples great teachers have consecrated their classrooms as places set apart for something that transcends whatever course subject they might be teaching. Great teachers create community because their classrooms are sacred. Honor, respect, seriousness of purpose presumed. Aristotle (2002:175) said that "we are better able to contemplate those around us than ourselves, and their actions better than our own," thus classrooms become locations not only to learn about subject matters but also about "ourselves."

Friendships form much more commonly in the classrooms of great teachers and students, and both "seem to become even better people by putting the friendship to work and by straightening one another out, for they have their rough edges knocked off by the things they like in one another. Hence the saying '(you will learn) from what is good in the good'" (Aristotle, 2002:180). The teacher-student and students-teachers make this so. The teacher and the students will think more completely, no doubt, when they have other people to work with. Great teachers may do more summer reading but probably less actual contemplation than they do during the school year due to that exercise of friendship toward students.

Classrooms become respites for the camaraderie celebrated by the existentialist, Albert Camus. They are places to forge identities and set new aspirations, and where better than in the classroom of a great teacher? Jean Paul Sartre emphasizes the need for others for learning and growth to take place. Edmund Burke (1988:218) argues the importance of all opinions for testing out the veracity of any proposition of truth. "I have never yet seen any plan which has not been mended by the observations of those who were much inferior in understanding to the person who took the lead in the business."

At their most transcendent best, great teachers' classrooms seem to validate the claims of Martin Buber (1958:45) that God is found in I-Thou, relationships where there is a shared center of being. "The true community . . . arise(s) . . . first, through (people) taking their stand in living mutual relations with a living Centre, and second, their being in living mutual relation with one another." Although this is a secular book, if Buber is correct, God may, then, find you in the great teacher's classroom.

Curiously the accounts of great teachers tend to neglect what fuels their respective fires. The dedication to students offers prima facie evidence that these teachers respond to an inner vision that emphasizes commitment to others. Whether such a commitment comes from an existential sense of duty or a belief in some form of the good, such as beauty, truth, justice, and virtue, great teachers' lives testify to the worth and value of something beyond the self.

Spitwad Sutras honors a particular teacher who finds his work as teaching the soul to be sublime. Robert Inchausti (1993) writes of a great and inspiring teacher, a Brother Blake. Inchausti (161) finds that "the best teachers are not those who amaze us with their eloquence or arrest our imaginations with their brilliance or even get us to work without our noticing it. They are those who reveal some realm of existence previously unknown to us and thereby redeem us from our forgetfulness and lost sublimity."

Inchausti's is the rare report of the great teacher's revealing his guiding lights, in this case Blake's search for lost sublimity. On the basis of his regard for Brother Blake, Inchausti (1993:151) observes that "there are many ways to teach successfully, but there is only one pedagogy of the sublime. This prophetic art is born of poetry, excess, exaggeration, and risk. It is not so much a means of instruction as it is a call to self-transcendence, an act of liberation."

Perhaps, even probably, none of the other great teachers of this study has identified the search for the sublime as the guiding light of their great teaching, but the example of Brother Blake intimates that great teachers have found some transcendent value that propels their teaching interests beyond their particular subject matter.

LIMITATIONS AND CLARIFICATIONS ABOUT GREAT TEACHING

Any great teacher you may have studied and used the same approach will not work for you. If you design units around dinosaurs like Jonathan Kozol, or performing Shakespeare plays like Rafe Esquith, you will most likely fail. Emerson asks, "Who is the man who can teach Shakespeare?" Only your students can teach you what works for you with them. No teacher-proof curricula exist.

Certainly some classroom practices offer greater prospects than others; start with those. But greatness lies in matching all that you might find to try with what inspires and helps students to learn. (However, a hint: When Jim Herndon decided that he wanted to make a movie in a class he was teaching, his formerly reluctant students eagerly joined in. It was not the movie; it was the genuineness of Herndon's enthusiasm.)

Sylvia Ashton-Warner documented her greatness as a teacher of Maori children in her book, *Teacher*, and then her subsequent trials in reproducing such success in an urban American school. Great teaching is always situational.

Inherently all students of a class are not equally ready for a course's challenges. Different capabilities. Different levels of previous preparation. The great teacher (not limited to and by so-called best practices) helps all students respond to the challenge without succumbing to fear and frustration. The key: challenge the student leaders, prop up the bottom, the middle will tend to go with the flow. Other than in tutorials great teaching requires momentum from the entire class.

The biblical admonition requires one to *love*, not *like*, others. Great teachers work for their students' best long-term interests; great teachers find the redeemable in each and every student; great teachers try to like all of their students because they are their students; great teachers pretend to like everyone and do so convincingly. Great teachers realize that the problem with that problem student is often related to something that they do not like about their own lives. Something about that student, if the teacher ponders the why, is that the student reminds them of something they do not like about themselves, or some close, significant other.

An outsider might not recognize the connection between the problematic student and the teacher's own personal issues, but it is usually there. The student who thinks she or he knows how the class should really be run may be amusing to one teacher and incredibly offensive to the teacher who has overcome family social pressures for conformity to try to be a great teacher. Any potential dislike of such a student becomes muted by the realization that it is not really the student who is disliked, but something about oneself.

Noted historian and great teacher, David Tyack, once observed in class that he thought that the quality and importance of teaching was inversely correlated with grade level, that the best teaching necessarily took place in kindergarten, and the worst could be gotten away with at the advanced doctoral level. At least a part of his point was that the kindergarten teacher had to consider the very most of the student as a person, and the professor the least about the student as a person. (Perhaps Tyack's repeated winning of the Teacher of the Year Award belied his position?)

Sylvia Ashton-Warner was a great teacher of infant school children, Rafe Esquith of elementary school children, Jim Herndon of junior high students, Jaime Escalante of high school students, David Tyack of college students. Ashton-Warner might have had to take a student to the toilet, Esquith taught students about manners in restaurants, Herndon created a school within a school. Escalante spent his Saturdays helping his students prepare for the Advanced Placement Calculus exam, Tyack took his dog to his office but had his colloquia at his home. In one sense each great teacher was personal and personable, but necessarily, as students individuate and become truly independent and each school level ordinarily necessitates being somewhat less personal. How personal should a great teacher be? The students and great teacher negotiate this relationship.

If a tree falls in a forest and no one is there, did it make a sound? This study makes a distinction between the great teacher and great teaching. Jaime Escalante was undoubtedly still a great teacher with his adult night school classes, but his greatest teaching was in relationship with particular students at a particular place, focusing on calculus. He only had all the requisites for great teaching at Garfield High School. He had the moxie, an ideal match of subject matter, personal talent, student needs, enough support (barely) to overcome the systemic obstacles . . . and enough recognition and enough time to make a difference for his students.

Conversely, a Professor Pearce at Occidental College in the late 1960s may have been a great teacher, but as an adjunct faculty member he never had the institutional clout to command the students' attention and establish his great teaching effectively. Great teachers need the opportunity, the match of subject and students, enough time, the place, and at least barely enough support to produce great teaching and, thus, great learning.

Finally, high expectations that lead to some students' great success will also bring up the bottom of the class. Jay Mathews was impressed that even those students of Jaime Escalante's who did not earn a passing grade on the Advanced Placement Calculus exam had profited by having met the challenge of Escalante's math program.

THE ENCOURAGING EXAMPLES OF PETE DIXON AND BEN JIMENEZ

To a much more limited extent this study has also considered fictional great teachers. Whatever the reality of such depictions, they inherently suggest what their creators wanted from these teachers. From television *Mr. Peepers*, *Our Miss Brooks*, the *Bill Cosby Show* (where he was a PE teacher), *The White Shadow*, *Welcome Back Kotter*, *Room 222*, *Ding Dong School*, *Mr. Wizard*, and *Fame* and films like *Goodbye Mr. Chips*, *Stand and Deliver*, *Music of the Heart*, *Mr. Holland's Opus*, *Dangerous Minds*, *Fast Times at Ridgemont High*, *Dead Poet's Society*, *Paper Chase*, *School of Rock*, *Teachers*, *The Man without a Face*, *To Sir, with Love*, and *Why Shoot the Teacher?*, each offer numerous images of teachers, including some great ones.

Pete Dixon of *Room 222* was something of a prototype for great teaching. Mr. Dixon also had the great fortune of having the support of his principal, Mr. Kaufman, and the school counselor, Liz McIntire. Dixon had developed a heroic persona. Whatever the costs, he would do the right thing. Mr. Kaufman might sometimes complain how difficult that heroism made his life as a principal, but by the end of the half hour he would shake his head and know that Dixon had done what he thought best, and Kaufman would protect him.

In one episode Mr. Dixon had been teaching Thoreau's *Civil Disobedience*. When he arrived in class the next day, the classroom was empty. Mr. Kaufman came down to the classroom in a huff. The students had left the school grounds and were picketing by an old tree that had been scheduled for being cut down for a new construction project. Mr. Kaufman protested that Dixon's class could not be involved in such demonstrations on school time; Dixon did not disagree, but he queried Kaufman about what he expected when students read great literature. How does the fictional Pete Dixon rate in terms of the criteria of this study?

Great teachers develop a persona, which is consistently heroic in some way and insistent on doing the right thing, believe that all students can succeed, offer leadership, have the voice of high expectation and commensurate deep concern for students, and stare down their own failures (one program devoted itself to Dixon's considering quitting and taking a higher-paying job outside of teaching). Dixon creates the persona of being both tough and challenging. He recognizes that the curriculum must also be about life, and that its hidden curriculum is about students taking on responsibility.

Dixon evidences that teachers use their classrooms as labs where the unexpected will happen, where he thrives (and the plots thrive) on his making quick changes in his plan to teach and inspire his students, particularly his problematic students. He uses that school experience to create a greater sense of community, which at times, perhaps, may lead students to take on their own social causes. He undertakes the *hows* of great teaching.

Specifically, how does he measure up on Peterson's characteristics?

For five seasons Mr. Dixon "had no fear of feeling and did not attempt to achieve that specious academic objectivity that can freeze a class." Quite the contrary. He had to accept that his students made an independent choice to demonstrate off the school grounds instead of being in school, a choice that he assured Mr. Kaufman was not one that he wanted them to make.

Mr. Dixon evidenced week after week that he had a thorough knowledge of his subject, history, bringing up relevant anecdotes from that history that consistently shed light on the issues at hand—likewise for his use of just the right example, whether metaphor or story. While he was also the most polished teacher at the high school, he was consistently challenged to work through issues like the students cutting school to demonstrate and what any punishment might be, demonstrating a "penetrating intelligence at work." He was intellectually challenging, and he prepared his students to go on to places like Harvard, but he was also just as supportive of the student with pushy parents and who did not have the skill set or aspirations to go there.

Even the principal looked to Pete Dixon. He had that gravitas that led others to seek out his opinion. While his persona was actually a little stuffy and his personality had to be brought out by the counselor and his love interest, Liz McIntire, he used his commanding presence to good effect. Mr. Dixon seemingly never intended to be insubordinate to Mr. Kaufman, but it was a good thing that the wise principal was willing to overlook such infractions of the school rules because students were doing what seemed right instead of always following those rules. In one episode Dixon helped return to a store a coat that had been stolen by a student rather that have the student face the consequences of being caught by the authorities. Such examples punctuate that he had broken down the insulation between student and teacher.

Mr. Dixon had one eye on his classroom but the other on his local community, and the larger society. He established respect through, not despite, his willingness to confront students with the implications of their choices. All his students were candidates for his intervention as needed, and he could even positively influence the "outlaw" student, Jason. He awakened students to talent they did not necessarily know that they had. He generated enthusiasm and responsibility among his students such that they would start look-ing out for one another. He created an atmosphere for learning. The script-writers' understanding of great teaching mirrors that of Houston Peterson's. (The television series holds up surprisingly well, and episodes are available on DVD.)

If the great teacher has the charisma of a Tom Cruise or Julia Roberts, perhaps that makes the great teacher easier to identify more quickly. Joe Cattarin, Caleb Clanton, and David Holmes are great teachers who have the magnetic personalities that inspire students to otherwise unexpected heights. Jaime Escalante had a charismatic personality and an extremely special pro-gram to teach. The same is true for Dave Levin of the KIPP schools (docu-mented in Jay Mathews's book, *Work Hard. Be Nice.*).

But both Escalante and Levin partnered with less charismatic, but similar-ly effective, teachers, who in fact were the truer inspiration for this study. Ben Jimenez also made major contributions to Garfield High School's Calcu-lus Advanced Placement program started by Jaime Escalante. Jay Mathews reports that Jimenez did so sometimes to greater success than Escalante with certain students. These students apparently resonated more soundly with Jimenez's quieter approach to teaching-learning. The same for Dan Corcoran at the KIPP schools, who at first felt under the shadow of the more assertive Levin. Corcoran eventually realized that he had to teach in his own quieter way. He then realized his own outstanding results, and he was eventually recognized with his own national teaching award.

A nerdy, naive, first-year teacher at Overfelt High School in San Jose, California, turned out to be a great teacher. For forty years. Veteran teachers thought she would never be "with it" enough to relate to her inner-city students. Goodness, commitment, openness, and learning from her students proved the critics wrong. She was a great teacher who quickly created great teaching by her whole-hearted commitment to her students.

But for the aspiring great teacher without obvious charisma, something extra, something above and beyond, something special, certainly helps separ-ate the great teachers from the pack. Calculus for Escalante, Shakespeare for Esquith, the KIPP schools for Levin, Advanced Placement History for John M. Daly, basic reading for Dick Tingey, literacy for Paulo Freire, key vocab-ulary (and an especially fine book) for Sylvia Ashton-Warner. Presumably it will take some time and opportunity for the beginning great teacher to find a suitable niche for delivering great teaching: a yearbook, a team, international travel, preceptorials? Advice to the great teacher: be relevant, be creative, pay attention, and recognize opportunity.

For the seemingly quiet Ben Jimenez mentioned above, a great teacher met his great opportunity in partnering with Jaime Escalante. Jay Mathews asks and answers the question essential to this study. Are teachers like Esca-lante made or born? Certainly most of the great teachers identified herein had flair in their notably strong personalities. But that is not required for greatness. Thus Escalante's colleague, Ben Jimenez, becomes the more important example for the possibilities of being one of the great teachers.

The less likely, less obvious, thus perhaps the more truly exemplary great teacher, Ben Jimenez, may be the best role model for this book because he best demonstrates that teachers can find within themselves what it takes to become great. Jay Mathews (1988:98) found that Jimenez "could not control his classes." He "had been diverted" from his teaching intentions. But he soldiered on anyway and sought out Escalante's help.

Once Jimenez had consulted with Escalante and had become more competent with classroom management, Jimenez started having success on his own terms. He even had success with some students with whom Escalante had not had such success (Mathews, 1988:230). "Into the smaller Jimenez camp came a few methodical, shy youngsters who had not enjoyed the circus in (Escalante's class) . . . Jimenez had taken the Escalante method and remodeled it to suit his very different personality. He rarely bullied . . . But he was there . . . the young man immersed himself in his classes as much as Escalante did." His results became comparable to those of Escalante (Mathews, 1988:231–32). "In 1984 fourteen of his sixteen students passed with a grade of 3 or better. In 1985 it was thirty of thirty-four. In 1986, twenty-three of twenty-six" (271).

Jimenez's statistical success does not mean that he was successful with each and every student either. Eventually the students decide whether to buy into the great teacher's great efforts on their behalf. Jimenez "dropped seven of his fifty students after the first semester." Not everyone needs to learn calculus, but Escalante and Jimenez had to be convinced that it was a real choice, not a lack of hope on the part of such a student.

Mathews (1988:67) writes that Jimenez had become a great teacher "despite his shyness" and in his own way. He shared Escalante's enthusiasm, but he retained his basic, more quiet personality. The argument here is that Jimenez was a great teacher from the beginning. Mathews (127) notes that Jimenez had the "same enthusiasm as when he started." He was a great teacher who matured into great teaching.

Thus, Mathews asks (291), "Are teachers like Escalante (and Jimenez) made or born?" Mathews concludes that "Jimenez' own talents are unusual enough to suggest some innate quality present long before (his teaching at Garfield High School) . . . that may be true of most good teachers, but some key skills can be learned. Jimenez learned from Escalante how to control a class. That practical knowledge made a critical difference in the younger teacher's career." Jimenez's success proves that many of the methods that worked for Escalante can also work for individuals whose backgrounds and personalities match those of the average American educator.

Mathews concludes that "Jimenez' methods worked," but a truer statement is that both great teachers, Escalante and Jimenez, best matched their respective and particular talents with the students' needs in ever-changing ways that worked best for the respective students that each had.

WORDS OF WISDOM AND TIPS

As discussed in the section on existential dilemmas in chapter 4, great teachers make day-to-day decisions based on their history with a student and with a class. A student's tardiness, for example, may be tolerated one day, but not another. The great teacher looks for patterns and an accumulation of events and does not feel constrained by consistency. As Ralph Waldo Emerson says, "A foolish consistency is the hobgoblin of little minds."

Presumably all people have different sides to their personalities. Students are well versed at "working" their teachers. Students spend more time with each other than with any specific teacher, and in a wider variety of settings. Great teachers check their limited perceptions of students with the word on the street, not necessarily to reject their own impressions, but certainly to see their students in a larger perspective. As Rafe Esquith (2003:90) warns in *There Are No Short Cuts*, "I have learned that before I decide if a kid is truly special, I had better observe and listen to his peers."

Existentialists nominally reject any suffering that does not contribute to consciousness, but appropriate pain does lead to gain. Great teachers share Rafe Esquith's (2003:92) commitment that "growing from pain is definitely the hardest route to follow, and it is the one I chose." Great teachers are more easily dissatisfied. Anything less than excellence is seen as failure, or nearly enough so, that still other approaches are attempted. No pain, no gain.

How can great teachers tolerate so much pain, self-reproach, and self-defined failure? With resilience. As Esquith asserts (2003:97): "Battered and bruised, but not defeated."

Besides resilience, humor helps assuage the pain. In his later book, *Teach Like Your Hair's on Fire*, Esquith (2007:138) once again acknowledges the personal costs in struggling to make a difference with students, but he finds solace in self-perspective and in being able to laugh at himself. "Later that night, as I chuckled myself to sleep." Implicitly Esquith recommends relying upon one's sense of humor. Learning to laugh at oneself is consistently therapeutic.

Sylvia Ashton-Warner (1963:x) offers her own palliative: "When I was guilty of feeling sorry for myself, I spent a day paying extra attention to a kid in class whom I liked very much." Often the best advice when feeling the lowest is to avoid hiding out to lick one's wounds and taking in the breath of fresh air on the school campus. One is likely to run into the gamut of students and colleagues who lift one's spirit.

Ashton-Warner also has a wise observation about the reasons not to dredge up all of those study aids stored in teacher file cabinets that may have helped former students. The old stuff is never fresh, and somehow that shows. Ashton-Warner (1963:79–80) concludes that "we don't waste enough in school. We hoard our old ideas on charts to be used again and again like stale bread. Ideas are never the same again, even those of the masters, even if the only change is in our own mood of re-approach. Yet there's never a shortage of ideas if the stimulus is there. Waste old paper and waste the old pictures and waste the old ideas. It's tidier and simpler."

Using small groups can be a smart addition to the teaching repertoire. Worried that using small groups means that the students are not getting their information from the horse's mouth? Russell Gersten's research among that of others confirms that peer-mediated instructional techniques can help students improve their learning.

Great teachers must have some institutional support and must have a workable venue to create great teaching. A high school principal had to allow Alice Coleman and John Daly to teach Advanced Placement classes and to join forces in a combined program. It took a courageous principal to take Advanced Placement History away from another teacher and assign it to Daly. That principal, and certain other teachers, also had to put up with the scheduling problems and conflicts created by scheduling Coleman's and Daly's courses back to back. Jaime Escalante was in constant conflict with administrators who could not, or would not, make concessions that Escalante felt that he needed. Escalante's most successful years were the ones in which he was protected by his principal, Henry Gradillas. Great teachers need at least a modicum of diplomacy to gain the necessary opportunity for great teaching.

Coleman, Daly, and Escalante were undoubtedly fine teachers in other settings, but their particular greatness worked to its best advantage when teaching students who had not yet realized that they could succeed at the elevated level of academic performance, symbolized by the prospects of an Ivy League education. Great teachers work to position themselves in situations that best match their interests and talents with those of their students.

Lewis Owen was a brilliant lecturer, but his greatness was most evident in his seminar size classes. Robert Nisbet (in Epstein, 1981:72) reports quite the opposite of "Teggart of Berkeley," "whose light is brighter before several hundred students than it is before a handful." Great teaching requires more than just a teacher with the capacity for greatness; great teachers do need a proper platform. As mentioned earlier, this study accepts an Aristotelian distinction between great teachers and great teaching. Even great teachers need some level of support and opportunity as well as some match between their strengths and their assignments to affect great teaching.

Great teachers take risks and are prone to being unconventional. A young, promising great teacher, who had developed basic classroom management skills and did not otherwise write disciplinary referrals, did theatrically interrupt a class and write a referral, sending a student to her counselor for her unacceptable underperformance.

A quiet, perhaps "alienated" student has not participated in class? Conspire with that student. Privately and outside of class time arrange that that student will have the answer, which you will give her/him, to a question that will stump the rest of the class. The question-answer has to somehow be relevant to the course of the classroom discussion, has to be esoteric knowledge that someone, but not just anyone, would know. The conspiring student should wait, wait, wait, until a pregnant pause has passed, and when no one else has been able to come up with the answer, then simply provide the answer aloud, while otherwise maintaining the same aloof countenance and demeanor as before—no big deal. Marvelously fun to do.

More tips:

1. Read widely and read widely about teaching, but with a discerning eye, realizing that greatness remains elusive, rare, and new ideas must suit you and your approach to teaching.
2. "Steal" from anywhere ideas that might work for you.
3. The essential question: "Can I make this work?"
4. You help your students by taking care of yourself, too.
5. Do a gut check almost every day—have you connected with each student recently?
6. What else can I try with _____?
7. Accept the truth that the research confirms: overpreparation makes for inauthentic teaching. Make your class work, not forcing the details of your pre-prepared lesson.
8. "Different, not deficit."
9. Appreciate differences; diversify instruction.
10. Not one of your students is likely to end up with your same college degrees and credentials. Focus on what would you want all educated people to know about your subject. Teach less better.
11. Come to agreements with students and hold students accountable to those agreements until the agreements are modified or changed. For example, the amount of homework needed by individual students varies. If a student can earn top grades without doing all of the home-

work, permit it . . . at least until a top grade is no longer earned by that student. Another student wants to sit next to a best friend? Fine, until it interferes with either's learning.

12. Great teachers John M. Daly and Alice Coleman seemingly stayed angry with their underachieving Advanced Placement students for the two straight years of their combined programs. Not every great teacher can maintain that level of energy and expectation. Other great teachers limit their times for being angry to either broken agreements or truly shoddy work. They take a less angry position of simply telling students the truth about the quality of their work and its implications for the students' desired futures.

13. Your students have not had enough sleep? It's the middle of the week. Just after exams. Maybe the weather is too hot. Have your students sing and act out *The Grand Old Duke of York*. Make students stand up, sit down, and neither up nor down. Gets their blood flowing. Unexpected. Gets their attention. Proves you can and will try anything. Works every time. Well, maybe for someone else, but can you make it work? If you would enjoy making students do this regardless of their seeming reactions, you will have made it work. If not, it is, conversely, guaranteed not to work.

14. Do you have the patience to rule that everyone speak once before anyone speaks twice? Too artificial? Can you promote class discussion by having an inner circle of students who discuss, and an outer circle who listen? Or, too artificial? Great teachers resolve the problems in front of them and cobble together and/or invent devices that promise to yield the desired results.

15. Please note: When a great teacher like Robert Sexton announces to a new class that it will likely be the best class that they ever take, he is not being arrogant, and in fact is setting an example for the person who would be a great teacher. Great teachers more than anyone else realize all the reasons that they are not truly great, keenly aware of their limitations and failures. Nonetheless, they know that their job is in one way easier once they have established a reputation such that new students enter their classes with high expectations. But that strategy has its downside as well. A recognized great teacher then feels compelled to live up to his/her own inflated reputation, which is its own challenge. How does a great teacher motivate herself/himself each course, each year? A way, and an effective way, is simply to announce something like Sexton suggests, that this will be the best class ever, and then having to live up to such wild indiscretion, leaving yourself with no place to coast or to hide.

16. Future Baseball Hall of Fame manager Sparky Anderson told his new team: "You don't have to like me. You don't have to respect me. I'm here to earn your respect." Such is the stuff of great leadership, whether managing a baseball team or a classroom.

SETTING UP THE CURRICULAR MATERIAL

Great teachers have to have credibility, but they also have to "set up" their best lines, best ploys, best lessons, and in a way that best considers their particular audience. Thinking about how they are going to "pull off" something with a class can keep a great teacher preoccupied for days, which often keeps them from living in the moment while mulling over future possibilities. These reveries can frustrate their family and friends who realize that they don't quite have the full attention that the great teacher's students receive.

The curricular set-ups occur for everything out of the ordinary that the teacher wants to try. Mr. Daly had to pick the right person to throw out of class to send the right message to a class of underperforming students. How did Coach Beck come up with the idea to let his two college-bound nonathletes spend the last semester of their senior year painting the school mascot on the gym wall instead of compromising the success of any one of the teams in his class Olympics? Surely Professor Hawkinshire could never have had Stanford students play the game Capture the Flag as a final exam if he had not convinced the class that his was the most intellectually rigorous class that they might ever take.

The teacher who smashed a student's (previously damaged, but the class did not know this) cell phone with a large hammer when it seemed to have rung and interrupted class had to have perfect timing, the complicity of the one student with the cell phone, and to realize that he could never repeat this stunt in a subsequent class. Law professor Jim McGoldrick found that he had three sets of professional musicians in his class, and he had to have the perfect timing to make the first two interruptions of his class seem spontaneous when the students-musicians responded to his legal questions in song.

Every subject has some have-tos. How are they set up for maximum effect? Perhaps the teacher assures students that this will be on the final but that the class can power through it in twelve minutes if everyone pays careful attention. ("Who has a watch and can time us?") No ploy that works can be overused, but one of the most versatile is the "reasonable choice" between two alternatives. "You can watch the rest of the film, and pay attention, or we can break for a quiz." "If everyone in the class passes this the first time, we will not have the second exam." "A warning, this book starts slowly, but virtually everyone finds the payoff makes it worth it."

Since great teachers know that no material is teacher-proof, they set up all their special events like late-night show hosts set up their monologues. And as they teach they continue to act a lot like a late-night show host: they try to make their "guests" look good and keep things lively and moving with great ad-libs along the way.

Chapter Four

Considerations for Great Teachers

Chapter 4 especially invites the reader to peruse and choose. In using the classroom as a lab, the great teacher looks for things with which to experiment. This chapter has four sections for such consideration. The first clarifies the importance of "differential effects," a consideration that helps clarify why variety is a virtue in the teacher trying to make important differences for students. The second part considers some of the more obvious ways in which students are sometimes thought to be different. The third raises a number of ways to expand one's teaching strategies. The fourth considers some ideas that may help a teacher think outside the box in expanding teaching possibilities.

All four sections assume the advantages of the adage: Appreciate differences; diversify instruction. A way of approaching teaching that emphasizes the appreciation of differences would be to use the class as a lab, reacting imaginatively on behalf of the students. This approach is premised on the thought that "we are only different in the ways we are the same" and that, for example, something that has been found to work with gifted students just might work with another student. Thus the individual class experience is authoritative, not the research on what is generally true across populations of students.

A seemingly unassuming adjunct professor at Seaver College consistently had her division's highest student evaluations. Encouraged by her success with students, she went on for her PhD in Education from a highly ranked university and went on to become a very popular tenured professor at Seaver. During her doctoral program she was heard to remark, "Oh, I get it, they just want you to name what it is that you do." She did not suddenly, for example, start teaching at a higher cognitive level on Bloom's Taxonomy, she could just now use Bloom as a way of explaining what she had already been doing.

Great teachers do not have to name what it is that they do. If they came by their success by instinct, intuition, and experience, the results are with their students, not in naming their methods. Nevertheless, there are some "names," some places to look that might facilitate figuring out what to try next in making progress with a class full of students. This chapter introduces some promising perspectives by which to consider differential effects, potential important differences among students, ways to expand one's teaching repertoire, and teaching outside of the box.

DIFFERENTIAL EFFECTS OF KNOWN SCHOOL VARIABLES THAT AFFECT SCHOOL OUTCOMES

This section discusses why "best practices" do not necessarily work—invariably a class of thirty-five students is not necessarily representative of the whole, and even if it was, relying only on the best practice will most likely fail to work with student outliers.

> A student does not develop in discrete, unrelated pieces but rather grows as an integrated whole. (Pascarelli, 2005:7)
> We concluded (that) . . . the literature has little to say about the differential effects of (school) on values and attitudes for different kinds of students. (Pascarelli, 2005:324)
> Whether (school) have differential impacts remains one of the unexplored frontiers in the research on college effects on students. (Pascarelli, 2005:327)

Great teachers are talent scouts, especially finding talent where other teachers may have overlooked it, and finding previously unidentified capacities that may be cultivated in each student. Great teachers also look for difference makers for those students. Pascarelli recognizes that the research has "little to say about the differential effects . . . (on) different kind of students." While in truth most students pass through the classes of great teachers on pretty much the same route with which they started, the great teacher knows, often from personal experience, how a teacher and a class can have a profound effect on a particular student's educational aspirations and school future.

The accounts of great teachers like Levin, Corcoran, Escalante, and Jimenez are replete with such stories. Great teachers are widely recognized as difference makers, but not for doing the same thing for all students. More accurately, they find the particular difference makers for the individual students that they have.

POSSIBLE DIFFERENCES AMONG STUDENTS THAT MIGHT MAKE A DIFFERENCE

Traditional Student Roles

Jeffrey McLellan (1999) studied high schools and identified five common student roles: all around, studious, average, disengaged, deviant. The movie *The Breakfast Club* had the jock, the princess, the nerd, the kook, and the outlaw. Whatever the truth behind such characterizations, the great teacher 1) does not confuse them with the individual student; 2) keeps in mind such potential differences among students do exist and to take into consideration any factor that might be seen as an important difference that can be accommodated in making plans for the curriculum to meet the needs of each and every student.

The alienated students are often the most neglected. Teacher and author Jenny Gray says that the most difficult students cause the most teacher growth. That the "alienated" student is still in school is evidence of not having given up entirely. Lessons that include and involve that student promise to be some of the richest for the student and the teacher.

English Language Learners

Coleman and Goldenberg (2010:12, 13) recommend the following as useful practices:

1. English oral language is best taught through explicit, direct instruction and interactive approaches.
2. Interactive approaches provide opportunities for authentic communication.
3. Daily oral English language instruction that targets language acquisition is recommended, about forty-five minutes a day.
4. Students need to learn expressive as well as receptive language.
5. Grouping by proficiency level for ELD instruction may be helpful.

Great teachers retain their high expectations for learners of English as a second language. As Professor Hank Levin realized, watering down the curriculum for any student behind in grade level only sentences that student to falling further behind. Levin argues for an accelerated curriculum. Great teachers are already elevating student expectations. Great teachers make a special point to engage these students in as many ways as possible.

They help such students brainstorm to find study aids. They consistently look for anything that might make their teaching better, and read materials like the list of useful practices above to consider as many strategies as possible. Having a second language has enormous potential advantages and can strengthen the first language, and students need to be encouraged to put in the extra time to accelerate learning.

Social Class Expectations (Working Class, Middle Class, Affluent Professional, Social Elite)

Jean Anyon's (1980) research found that schools for different social classes may teach the same subjects but do not do so in the same fashion. In a shorthand view, working-class students tend to do worksheets, middle-class students use the formulas and check their answers in the back of the book; affluent-professional students do creative projects; social-elite students read original material, discuss it, and write about it.

In a similar vein, working-class students expect rules and punishments; middle-class students are prodded by the guilt squeeze ("after all that I have done for you?"); affluent-professional students expect appreciation, recognition, and awards and a challenge to their pride; social-elite students expect to be treated as equals, except in terms of a teacher's curriculum expertise. Knowing those tendencies may be helpful in beginning to understand the atmosphere and expectations of a student, of a class, and of a school, but no teacher should presume that all students within a social class are consistent in the generalizations.

Great teachers work toward students of any social class learning to be as autonomous as possible. But perhaps if a nervous student would like the security of some worksheets, well, the argument here is that the great teacher does whatever is necessary to be successful with individual students.

Students with Disabilities

Robert Slavin (2009:399) offers the following tips for including students in the general classroom.

Teachers of students with learning disabilities should:

1. Specifically teach self-recording strategies, such as asking, "Was I paying attention?"
2. Relate new material to knowledge that the student with learning disabilities already has, drawing specific implications from familiar information.
3. Teach the use of external memory enhancers (for example, lists and note taking).
4. Encourage the use of other devices to improve class performance (for example, tape recorders).

Teachers of students with emotional or behavioral disorders should:

1. Create positive relationships within the classroom through the use of cooperative learning teams and group-oriented assignments.
2. Use all students in creating standards for conduct as well as consequences for positive and negative behaviors.
3. Focus their efforts on developing a positive relationship with the student with behavior disorders by greeting him or her regularly, informally talking with him or her at appropriate times, attending to improvement in his or her performance, and becoming aware of his or her interests.
4. Work closely with the members of the teacher assistance team to be aware of teacher behaviors that might adversely or positively affect students' performance.
5. Realize that changes in behavior often occur very gradually, with periods of regression and sometimes tumult.

Such suggestions as those above may very well work so well as to benefit all of the students in a class.

Perhaps one of the greatest challenges to schools of the past twenty-five years has been making the push for mainstreaming successful. Incredibly important. Nonetheless, American schools, especially the comprehensive high schools, historically developed along the lines of the factory model. Managing to place thirty-five students of about the same age group into a single class taught by one teacher was efficient and reasonably successful. Education achieved for less than the cost of child care. Accommodating differences is necessary, but not efficient.

John Goodlad's research found that teachers continue to be the center of attention in America's classrooms. A mainstreamed special education student or students are often a great challenge to the traditional ways of organizing teaching. Fortunately, research also indicates that peer-assisted teaching can be even more effective, so any changes in teaching approaches due to mainstreaming are most likely a very positive educational development. Great teachers were already making constant adjustments and changes because all of their students are special education clients. Slavin's tips above may not only be useful in aiding students with disabilities but also may work just as well for students who are not so classified.

Gardner's Multiple Intelligences

Gardner's theory of multiple intelligences implies that concepts should be taught in a variety of ways that call on many types of intelligence. (Slavin, 2009:8)

Howard Gardner (in Slavin, 2009) has identified eight separate intelligences. While they have not traditionally all been equally recognized and rewarded in school, developing strengths and shoring up weaknesses in types of intelligence in all of these areas seems the "smart" thing to do with regard to all students. Creating a learning community increases the likelihood that students who otherwise hang out only with those of a similar intelligence may find that when an assignment requires, for example, being "word smart," the word-smart student who is also music smart can help the music-smart person who struggles with this type of intelligence.

- Linguistic intelligence ("word smart")
- Logical-mathematical intelligence ("number/reasoning smart")
- Spatial intelligence ("picture smart")
- Bodily-kinesthetic intelligence ("body smart")
- Musical intelligence ("music smart")
- Interpersonal intelligence ("people smart")
- Intrapersonal intelligence ("self smart")
- Naturalist intelligence ("nature smart")

Great teacher Larry Giacomino has all of these intelligences. A Renaissance man. Reads literature and writes poetry; good at math and teaches science; has built his own home and boat and rebuilt his car; is a renowned mountain climber; writes and sings country songs (so this may be his one relative weakness?); his success as a teacher is founded more in his interpersonal and intrapersonal intelligence than even his great subject expertise (he's even a doctor); and he is a John Muir–loving naturalist who owns a cabin near Yosemite.

Fortunately, great teachers do not need to be great in all these areas. One will probably do, and that only needs to be good enough to commit to performing greatly on behalf of students. But great teachers would do well to help students of any set of intelligences excel at that teacher's subject matter.

Eventually the number of possible considerations for a class full of students would be too overwhelming except that the best advice remains to appreciate differences; diversify instruction; and check with students very often to see that they have found some way to get something out of all the lessons.

What's In a Name? Respecting Your Students' Understanding of Their Individual Ethnicities

Whatever the generalizations about names, ethnicity, religion, social class, or previous academic preparation, the advice here is to avoid using such categories or assigning such categories to your students. Your students will tell you what they want you to know about such matters, and at least some of them will most likely defy, and even resent, the generalizations about categories that they may or may not fit.

Great teachers are sensitive about "labels," not to be politically correct, but because in the public context of the classroom each student deserves sensitivity and respect. While a great teacher may very well think of herself as a lady, why would she want or need to use that term with regard to a group that might include those who find that term objectionable? White, Anglo, Caucasian? No such term is neutral; all such terms are potentially problematic in reference to any individual.

While the majority group is usually less sensitive about designation, why decide for anyone else? Race, religion, ethnicity, social class, stature, intelligence, and roles in school tend to make for categorization, which tends to make for stereotypes. Oriental is a carpet, Scotch an alcoholic drink, non-Catholic Christians do not necessarily see themselves as Protestants, your class may very well have African American students and black students and the children of undocumented workers.

Whatever their origins, terms like *m.r.* are highly pejorative; Dick Gregory's mother told him that they were broke, not poor; the TV program is titled *Big World, Little People*; and jockette is implicitly sexist whatever the intended humor. *Logos.* The world is created and recreated through language. If you asked someone her name and she answered Elizabeth, is it not presumptuous to call that person Beth on your own? Los Angeles Ram Lawrence McCutcheon told people not to call him Larry, that was his brother's name. Names have great emotive power beyond any denotation that they also carry.

Great teachers are sensitive, respectful, and careful. Is that particular person Caucasian, thus with ancestors from the vicinity of the Caucasoid Mountains? Anglo even though from Italy? Hispanic because of a grandmother from Spain? White, despite a rosy complexion? Anyone might appreciate reading Tim Wise's book, *White Like Me*, but meanwhile for the great teacher a student need not have a label unless s/he has given one that s/he has established as an important part of who s/he is.

Body Language

Understanding body language can be as, or more, complicated than understanding a "foreign" language. Mary John O'Hair and Eero Ropo (1994:91–111) identify five major components of body language. The five major components include: paralanguage (use of the voice including loudness and tone); facial expressions; eye and visual behavior (including eye contact and gaze); gestures and body movements; and space.

Do great teachers read body language better than most, or do they just spend more time figuring out what it means? The otherwise same example of body language can mean very different things. Even today in major league baseball a player from the Dominican Republic may make an error and smile, and one fan will conclude that the player obviously does not care, does not take the error seriously, and boo him, while another, less vociferous fan, will recognize that this player is showing embarrassment.

Raise one's voice with a student and the lesson is that the teacher does not care for that student, yet the same tone with another student proves that the teacher does care. Smile at a student? Was it flirtatious? Intimidating? Condescending? Perhaps a great teacher wants students to stand up to her. Is direct eye contact a sign of respect or disrespect? Was patting a student on the head a sign of appreciation or was it condescending? Is moving close into a student's space a sign of familiarity or an invasion of privacy?

Such matters as these are the reasons that a book can suggest questions to ask and places to look, but only your students individually have the answers to these questions. The key is the willingness to use the classroom as a lab and learn to read the body language of the class's students.

Female and Male

When Flo Jo (Florence Joyner) was running sprints in the Olympics, out of about three billion men on the planet only about 187 ran as fast as she did. Whatever differences there may or may not be between male and female students, you will not likely have a random distribution in your small classroom. As an example, quite possibly the fastest person in the class will be a female, even though men continue to hold the world records.

What about the "fact" that men purportedly do better in math? That "fact" tends to go away when researchers control for how many math classes the respective students took. If math has historically been a male subject and women are so close in performance anyway, an equally plausible conclusion is that women are better at math. For the great teacher, it does not matter. Any generalization that could be proven to be true for a normal distribution of people does not guarantee that your class has a normal representation.

Having said all of that, there has been discussion in the educational literature for the past few years that schools have become more female friendly and male unfriendly of late. If historically women students have been more willing to get with the program and male students to work independently, such a trend may be a disservice to both females and males.

American schools have often been better regarded outside of the United States than within. A reason has been thought to be their emphasis, especially at the college and university levels, on creativity, independent thought, and critical and divergent thinking. If schools are increasingly rewarding the amount of work instead of rigor, conformity instead of originality, compliance instead of challenge, then the future of America is not well served. It is not an issue anyway for great teachers of female or male students.

POTENTIAL TEACHING STRATEGIES

The Basics of Curriculum and Teaching

Objectives, teaching activities, organization of those teaching activities, and evaluation are the mainstays of public instruction, but they offer no prescriptions for the great teachers. (Parenthetically, great teachers are concerned with "teaching," not the more pedestrian "instruction," and the word *training* is anathema—seals are trained, students are educated.)

A meta-analysis of the research on the writing of objectives has not found that writing objectives tends to improve student learning. With regard to teaching activities, most great teachers vary their methods, but great teachers Joe Cattarin of Half Moon Bay High School and Richard Gross of Stanford University somehow thrived on straight lectures. Organization of teaching activities? While chronology, or simple to complex, for example, might be places to start in curriculum development, the great teacher adjusts the plans to reach the students, however unorthodox the organization might seem superficially.

Evaluation? Students do well on tests that measure what they were taught. But great teachers know that students learn many more lessons than can be measured. Great teachers try to make evaluation meaningful and fair. Great teachers do not hide behind a system or behind points. The great teacher is the measure, and he or she knows that there is more than one way to be great. Pablo Picasso, Blue Corn, Gordon Parks; Miles Davis, Ludwig van Beethoven, John Lennon; Akira Kurosawa, Jane Campion, Steven Spielberg; Toni Morrison, William Faulkner, Chinua Achebe. As Norvel Young has observed, there is no competition among lighthouses.

Too many educational initiatives of recent years have tended to standardize at the expense of setting high standards. Many students' academic careers have been dependent upon the grace of their great teachers emphasizing their best work and treating their lesser work with more than a little grace. In statistics the data tends to be more stable if one lops off the top 5 percent and the bottom 5 percent of the data. Great teachers, perhaps, are prone to keep the top 5 percent but ignore the bottom, which was simply practice toward getting better.

In addition, the longer the syllabus the less likely the students are to read it. The tendency of the long and detailed syllabus is to tie one's hands instead of leaving room to use the class as a lab where things may change.

Motivation

The following are factors in motivation (from Gage's *Educational Psychology* in Gose, 1999:86–87):

1. Use verbal praise.
2. Use tests and grades judiciously.
3. Capitalize on the arousal value of suspense, discovery, curiosity, and exploration.
4. Occasionally do the unexpected.
5. Whet the appetite.
6. Use familiar material for examples.
7. Use unique and unexpected contexts.
8. Require use of what has previously been learned.
9. Use simulations and games.
10. Minimize the attractiveness of competing motivational systems.
11. Minimize the unpleasant consequences.
12. Understand the social climate of the school.
13. Understand the power relationships between teachers and students.

Great teachers are great motivators. They probably use most of the factors identified by Nate Gage and Dave Berliner above. They also motivate by cajoling, badgering, hassling, kidding, needling, picking on, challenging, bribing, daring, betting, pestering, haranguing, teasing, demanding, using the guilt squeeze, scolding, withholding affection, and any other number of seemingly less kind motivational ploys that work when the students clearly feel and experience the teacher's underlying concern and caring.

On understanding the social climate of the school: often the great teacher has to establish a climate that might otherwise be lacking at the school. That might include a willingness to work co-operatively, to set higher educational aspirations, to increase time spent on homework, and to improve attendance. Research suggests that students' diffuse peer group particularly influences their educational aspirations. Not the immediate peers, but those whom the student may only know by name. The peer group has a greater influence on day-to-day decisions, but the diffuse peer group influences the aspirations.

Thus for even any precollege teacher who wants to encourage his or her students to become college bound, compensating for the lack of support in the students' larger social circle may be a critical need to fill. The great teacher pays special attention to the social climate. For example, the 2002 book by Anthony S. Bryk and Barbara Schneider, *Trust in Schools*, documents the connection between relationships at a school and students' academic achievement.

Authority

N. L. Gage identifies five forms of authority that are potentially available to all teachers: reward, coercive, legitimate, referent, and expert (in Gose, 1999:87). By the end of a course a great teacher expects to have established referential respect. Why else be a great teacher? But great teachers do what is necessary to earn that respect, including, as necessary, the use of rewards and threats. If authority is questioned (in contrast to challenged) the great teacher might resort to legitimate power and make a phone call home, send the student to the office, assign detention, or to exert authority: "There's nothing particularly wrong with your paper, so much as it lacks robustness." As discussed in the first chapter about Ben Jimenez, great teaching must be built upon basic classroom management skills. Establishing authority over a class is absolutely essential, and attention to each of these five sources of authority may be helpful.

The Importance of Teaching Reading and Study Skills

A major consideration of chapter 3 is that great teachers use their classes as laboratories, experimenting to find what works best with that class. A critical factor for any teacher, not just great teachers, is to teach students the reading skills necessary to be successful with the teacher's subject matter. Math texts are consistently written at a reading level higher than the math level; textbooks are consistently written at higher levels than the grade to which students are assigned. Texts are written for the kind of people who already have that particular kind of intelligence, not for those with other kinds of intelligence (see the section on Gardner and multiple intelligences).

Educators have recently been calling such help for students, including requisite reading skills, as "scaffolding." Whether it is how to use the Internet to find certain kinds of information, how to take notes, how to differentiate between connotation and denotation, or how to organize time, great teachers set aside time to teach the skills, especially the reading and study skills, necessary for students to succeed at higher levels.

The *Chronicle of Higher Education* Recommendations

Ken Bain (2004:B7) studied sixty professors from various disciplines and created his own list of practices that make teachers great. Bain asked, "What do any of the best professors do to encourage students to achieve remarkable learning results?" He especially found that they "create a natural learning environment (and) ask probing and insightful questions (which was) by far the most important principle."

In emphasizing questions, Bain found that "an intriguing question or problem is the first (element) that makes up a good learning environment." He emphasized "guidance in helping students understand the significance of the question." He found that great teachers "embed the discipline's issues in broader concerns, often taking an interdisciplinary approach." Bain found that great teachers "remind students how the current question relates to some large issue that already interests them." They "engage students in some higher-order intellectual activity" and "help students help themselves answer the question." Finally, Bain observes that the great teachers "leave students wondering: What's the next question? and What can we ask now?"

Bain's (2004:B7) tips for great teachers include:

1. Get students' attention and keep it.
2. Start with the students rather than the discipline.
3. Seek commitments.
4. Help students learn outside of class . . . helps build a sense of community . . . encouraging students to learn on their own, engaging them in deep thinking.
5. Engage students in disciplinary thinking.
6. Create diverse learning experiences.

The *Chronicle of Higher Education* understandably limits Bain's discussion of "what makes great teachers great" to college and university professors. Such professors have the good and bad fortune of having much more conscribed teaching hours. By virtue of the more irregular meeting times, the self-selection that goes with which students choose to go to college, and an even greater emphasis in higher education on academic disciplinary study, focusing primarily on the questions raised in a class seems especially relevant to college teaching.

Certainly great teachers at any level can and do profit from emphasizing questions (and for their students to learn to generate their own quality questions [Gose, 2011]), and it is refreshing to find such a journal advocating starting with the students rather than the discipline and to use diverse learning experiences despite what seems to be a continuing emphasis on lecture at the college level. Generating quality questions is characteristic of great teachers, but it is only one of the many ways that great teachers create learning communities.

The *Chronicle of Higher Education* finds that great teachers create diverse learning experiences. Great teachers find what works for them with their students in their sort of class. Somewhere along the line most teachers have been exposed to all of the following methods and could probably use them with but a little extra preparation. Bruce Joyce has found that teachers can learn new models of teaching, and if called upon to use a newly learned model sometime later, can do it again. But unless there is institutional support for using different methods, they will not use the new methods. Great teachers do what works, but they do not use any of these methods for diversity's sake, or in an artificial manner. The key is whether it is helpful as a vehicle with these students on this particular day.

One "method" not on the list of teaching strategies that follows and that encourages asking probing questions is putting a student "on the hot seat." If all students know that they will be on the hot seat, they accept the odd assignment, and by the teacher asking process questions instead of factual questions, it can push each student one at a time to consider the ins and outs of the studied subject. Putting yourself on the hot seat in terms of great teaching, perhaps, why would you want to be a great teacher? What might stop you? What are the probable costs? What might best help you in this regard? Who might help you? What readings suddenly make sense? Will you likely have similar ideas in five years, ten years, and twenty years? The hot seat might help each student to forthrightly personalize and better understand the concomitant issues.

A List of Teaching Strategy Possibilities

There are a great variety of potential teaching strategies that might be best matched with students' learning styles and needs. The great teacher determines which are to be tried with particular subjects and particular classes, but "generally" (a word used cautiously), diversity offers some spice to life.

Case study	programmed learning
Contracting	Projects
Demonstrating	Questioning
Discovery	Role-playing
Discussion	Small groups
Drill	Simulations
Field trips	Socratic dialogue
Independent study	Student research
Individualized learning	Tutoring
Learning centers	Team teaching
Learning packets	Using various media
Lecture	Using students' strengths
Observation	and propping up their weaknesses
Problem-solving	

When you are looking for a new ploy, the list might suggest the type of activity to try.

Curriculum Development

This section on curriculum development is included because of the artistry often practiced by great teachers in the creation of their curricula:

> Trying to make it real compared to what.
> It looks like we always end up in a rut.
> Trying to make it real compared to what!
> —Les McCann, jazz musician, *Live at Montreaux*

Academy Award winner for best actor, Rod Steiger, visited an undergraduate film class. In discussing his best actor performance nomination in *The Pawnbroker* and his ineffable scream at the film's end, Steiger told the class that the image that entered his mind in this one-take scene was that of Pablo Picasso's famous antiwar painting, *Guernica*. Steiger then encouraged the class to learn absolutely as much as possible about everything because you never knew what might enter your mind to inspire you.

This powerful "lesson" may not have been a part of "prescribed objectives" for the course, but as Elliot Eisner (*Educational Imagination*) has suggested, the students could after the fact be asked to "express the outcomes" of this educational encounter with Steiger in ways that show meaningful learning. Steiger's recollection about his art suggests how nondiscursive ideas/images/pictures may also enter deliberations on how curriculum development can be an art medium.

While there has been some limited attention to the art of teaching in the professional literature, very little, if anything, has been written on the art of curriculum development. Certainly curriculum planning and development does not always reach the level of "art," but surely sometimes it ascends to those lofty heights of aesthetics.

The four senses of art that Eisner (1979:153–68) uses to describe teaching as art suggest that 1) how curriculum work can be so well conceived that it is truly aesthetic; 2) that "qualitative judgment is exercised in the interests of achieving a qualitative end"; 3) that the curriculum has to have those qualities of both repertoire and inventiveness to allow the person who teaches the curriculum to make it an artistic experience; and 4) that the ends of the planning are emergent, not entirely preconceived and prespecified. Curriculum development has the capacity to generate such aesthetic experience.

Aesthetic pleasure and accomplishment can occur in the planning of individual lessons, units, courses, frameworks, and programs. The teacher's notepad on which curriculum plans are made can become the canvas of artistic expression. Perhaps such artistic ideas seem "soft" in the face of the rigor one can use in implementing national curriculum efforts, state frameworks, new textbooks with accompanying teacher guides, professional work by time-honored scholars such as Hilda Taba and Ralph Tyler, and cutting-edge ideas based on research.

Curriculum artists need not ignore the contingencies, perspectives, databases, and research findings in conducting curriculum planning and development. Certainly the word *curriculum* brings to one's mind Ralph Tyler's four questions from *Basic Principles of Curriculum and Instruction*: questions about the goals, teaching strategies, organization of the teaching strategies, and evaluation. But there are countless other ideas well able to inform curriculum planning and development. Ideas associated with Eisner, Noddings, Shaftel, Ashton-Walker, Freire, Giroux, Jackson, Apple, Bloom, Bruner, Piaget, Gage, Berliner, Dewey, and more are all at the beck and call of the curriculum developer.

The Steiger comment suggests the role that memory and intuition might play to animate, to inspire curriculum making. Two motifs or artistic impressions have special import for curricular deliberations. Metaphorically, Les McCann's song, "Compared to What," with its keyboard, electric bass, American drums, African drums, the jazz, and particularly its refrain, "Trying to make it real compared to what!" suggest a vision for rich, creative design that brings the curriculum to life and makes it more real.

Of course, any academic work in a classroom has artifice about it, but the curriculum can at least be made "real compared to what." The curriculum can be made more "real" than the mere words in the textbook. By using guests, field trips, examples from television, the movies, the newspapers, websites, role-playing, simulations, anecdotes, and more, the curriculum can be made more real, more vibrant, more alive than the (invaluable, indispensable) printed texts and lectures. Inherently the music of Les McCann challenges the teacher to make the curriculum as real as feasible.

Another potential influence on curriculum development comes from Impressionism and the images of Impressionistic paintings. Particularly paintings such as those Monet completed in London suggest a way of conceptualizing curricular work. The curriculum becomes an important view of the subject. Like Monet the curriculum planner has to frame what will be studied. The canvas itself must create a vivid impression of that subject matter. The vision must be comprehensible, responsible to the subject, vivid, memorable.

The curricular artistry is not the same as reality, but someone else, someone knowledgeable about the subject, would be expected to be able to recognize the material as a captivating impression of the whole. Invariably, there is something "superficial" about the representation, yet the portrayal captures something authentic about what the artist has viewed and presented, in this case to students. Monet also said that when he quit working on the canvas as a whole, he quit working, an apt "lesson" for curriculum developers so that the overall effect is always kept in mind.

Likewise, in any curriculum work the teacher does expect the student to have an overview, a full impression of the field being studied. Taken together the brilliant strokes will create a captivating and lasting impression of the field as a whole. The treatment will be authentic. Besides learning the material, the students will have a sense of aesthetic pleasure in having viewed this curriculum.

Certainly creating such an aesthetic view of important academic subject matter does not preclude the more obvious aspects of curriculum planning. The teacher will still most likely define the objectives, identify the teaching methods to be used, organize those methods for effect, and plan formal evaluations. The more logical and deliberate aspects of curriculum planning remain in place. However, after the creation of such work, should not the last act be to stand back from the creation to see whether the overall impression is pleasing and hopefully lasting?

Making Groups Work

Great teachers solve the problems at hand. Sometimes the paramount problem is the failure of the class to work together effectively. Perhaps one or more of the students is dominating, or too many students do not participate fully. Giving them the opportunity to critique their own group performance at a common task can alter the class's future behavior. "A" method of setting up such an experience: place students in groups of four and have them create a list of ten Hollywood films that have the most implication for the class's subject matter (for example, *Stand and Deliver* for math, *Shakespeare in Love* for English, *An Inconvenient Truth* for science might make respective lists).

Since no student has a definitive answer for this assignment, all group members will likely participate and think of a film that the others neglected. The key to the exercise is to assign a fifth student to each group to observe the group process. After the groups' lists are completed, the observers debrief the entire class on what kinds of behaviors were observed, including the constructive and not so constructive, based upon the following roles and behaviors. The class awareness of these roles and behaviors can be eye opening for them and work to resolve a problem hampering the class. (Adapted from Hunter, 1972.)

The following list of group roles are divided into three parts: behavior that furthers the work or talk of the group, behaviors that maintain the group as a smoothly functioning unit, and personal-oriented behaviors that interfere with the work of the group.

Group Task Behavior: Conduct That Furthers the Work of the Group

1. Initiating—proposes, aims, leads, actions, or procedures
2. Informing—ask for or offers facts, ideas, feelings, or opinions
3. Clarifying—illuminates or builds upon ideas or suggestions
4. Summarizing—pulls data together, so group may consider where it is
5. Consensus testing—explores whether a group may be near a decision; prevents premature decision making

Group Maintenance Behavior: Conduct That Helps the Group Function Productively

1. Harmonizing—reconciles disagreement, relieves tension, helps people explore differences
2. Gate keeping—brings others in, suggests facilitating procedures, keeps communication channels open
3. Encouraging—warm and responsive; indicates with words or facial expression that the contributions of others are accepted
4. Compromising—modified position so group may move ahead; admits error
5. Gives feedback—reflects the feeling of the group, gives impression to users of self-oriented behaviors

Personal or Self-Oriented Behavior: Conduct That Interferes with the Work of the Group

1. Aggressing—attacks, deflates, uses sarcasm
2. Blocking—resists beyond reason, uses hidden agenda items that prevent group movement
3. Avoiding—prevents group from facing controversial issues, stays off subject to avoid commitment
4. Dominating—interrupts, asserts authority, overparticipates to point of interfering with others' participation
5. Abandoning—makes an obvious display of lack of involvement
6. Deferring (to authority or aggressors)—differs his/her opinion or suggestion in the face of criticism from others, does not clarify her/his position for the group
7. Verbally passive—nonverbal cues say that the person is participating nonverbally (eye contact, nodding, smiling, "un-uhing") but does not interject his/her own thoughts (or agreements, disagreements) verbally
8. Personalizes—frequently uses personal anecdotes that detract from the group task

Observation Sheets for Group Task Behaviors

	1.	2.	3.	4.	5.	6.	7.
Group Task Behavior							
1. Initiating							
2. Informing							
3. Clarifying							
4.Summarizing							
5.ConsensusTaking							
Group Maintenance Behavior							
1. Harmonizing							
2. Gate Keeping							
3. Encouraging							
4. Compromising							
5. Giving Feedback							
Personal or Self-Oriented Behavior							
1. Aggressing							
2. Blocking							
3. Dominating							
4. Avoiding							
5. Abandoning							
6. Deferring to Authority							
7. Verbally Passive							
8. Personalizes							

Observer's Name

_____

A Method for Assessment

Great teachers tend to distrust anything standardized because they are looking for subtle differences by which to tailor their efforts. A great way to find
out how students are responding to the curriculum is to ask them to write
down ten questions about an important course issue, topic, or reading; promise them that they will not be required to answer their questions; and read
what they have to ask.

Students usually have more thoughtful questions than their answers to
any quiz would suggest. The discerning teacher can find patterns among the
students' questions that help better appreciate how well the students are
relating to the curriculum. Overall, ten questions seem to be a good number,
although some students may not finish with ten. Generally the first couple of

questions are starter questions and not all that interesting, and the last questions may be throwaways, but by writing ten, the middle questions are often quite revealing.

Improv

Teachers may have as much to teach about "improv" as drama teachers. Some of the lessons associated with improv well apply to the great teachers. For example, "Failure is an option." A lack of failure would be its own evidence that the teacher has not pushed the edges of what might be most possible. Recognizing the class as a lab, great teachers learn from their mistakes. Successful improv usually requires going with one's gut, which great teachers do better than most already. Improv emphasizes "reaction," and great teachers have a "wittiness" that allows them to respond accurately, creatively, and meaningfully to their students.

Improv emphasizes body language as well as the spoken word. Enhancing and clarifying body language can only improve teaching.

There are no prescriptions. The nature of improv is that it must be spontaneous, apt, and "work." The subject matter may dictate the classroom use for most of the classroom time, but the supporting minutes may be what sustain the necessary flow of classroom energy. A teacher might turn off the lights in reaction to something that happened in class, and make it work. The tip is not to try turning off the lights, the tip is to open one's imagination to any and all possibilities, tailoring (changing metaphors from "lab") one's teaching in the moment.

What can be done to the classroom to change the dynamics for a given moment or class? Where might the students be taken on a sudden field trip? Who might be invited to drop by virtually at a moment's notice? What might be distributed to students? nicknames? certificates? team shirts? How many ways might a student be approached? outside of class? after class? after school? a phone call? a home visit?

What sounds might be added to a classroom? What "street theater" (like bashing a student's phone that has again gone off in class, unbeknownst to the rest of the class that you are bashing a substitute phone that was already broken)? Great teachers spend time on the curriculum but also on the supporting possibilities that might be brought in through improvisation. Such activities are often necessary to sustain the momentum of the curriculum delivery. (For a scholarly article establishing the heuristic value of improvisational teaching, please see:

http://www.aera.net/uploadedFiles/Journals_and_Publications/Journals/ Educational_Researcher/Volume_33_No_2/2026-03_Sawyer.pdf.)

Summarizing many of the "lessons" of improv identified by Sawyer and others are the lessons of improv for effective teaching:

- Stay in the moment.
- React to a classroom event with "Yes, and . . ." rather than "Yes, but . . ." That is, stay positive and nonjudgmental often by repeating what a student has said and building upon it. If the student says, for example, "We should not have to take this class," instead of responding with, "Yes, but then look how ignorant you would be," say instead something like, "Yes, and the student desks should be more comfortable in the meantime."
- Failure is okay. Late-night show hosts often get their biggest laughs by their own reaction to the jokes that did not work.
- Listen. An advantage of the improv mind-set is that one recognizes the need to listen because one can never anticipate just what might come next.
- React. Great teachers learn to react spontaneously, without a script, and students respond to the freshness. The teacher has so much more knowledge about the subject that she or he can realize what best comes next.
- Humor is good. *USA Today* once reported that Americans only laugh about six times a day. A great teacher should elicit many more laughs than that every class period.
- Build up; do not tear down. Teacher educator Alfred Grommon convinced most of his student teachers that they should not use red ink grading papers. Constructive criticism builds up.
- Use your imagination; realize a much wider range of possible responses.
- Do you always use the same greeting? The same handshake? The same response to "how are you"?
- Use all aspects of body language. Great teachers' feet should be tired at the end of the day, not their voices. Movement, gestures, facial expressions, and voice modulations all complement the words that while necessary to teachers are overdrawn.

A problem with learning improv is that one cannot practice on one's own. Here are some exercises you might try if you can find a willing partner:

1. Brainstorm how many ways to say hello, goodbye, and use the word *poop* in ways that could be said on television.
2. Create a signature move with your body that is an alternative to saying your name. Respond to your partner's own signature move with a corresponding move that says, "Glad to meet you."
3. Make quick responses to your partner, asking any one of the following that students are likely to say or ask: this is boring; you are mean; will you go out with me; what's your first name; what kind of car do you drive; are you married; I hate math.
4. Practice "yes, and . . ." (then add something) to the items in #3 above.
5. Make a sound, have your partner make a sound, and go back and forth with new ones as long as possible.

6. Practice more "yes, ands . . .?" Respond to: What is the most outlandish thing you have ever done? (these do not have to be true), Of what are you most proud?, What was an embarrassing moment?, What's something most people don't know about you?, Can you tell a short joke?, What's the most dangerous thing you have ever done?, What would most people not believe about you?

7. Learn to appreciate failure. Find responses like, "that didn't work, did it?" and learn to appreciate that only by learning from failure can you truly expand your teaching capacities.

8. Demonstrate to each other: How much you love math? How you sit down to study? How does this class really makes you feel? What do you think of improv?

9. Stay in the moment with each other. Do not stick to a script, even this one. It's hard to do, but it is easier if you realize that it is not the hour you spent planning the lesson but the decades you spent being ready for the moment. Do not let Noman tell you otherwise; this is the stuff of authentic teaching, and, besides, it will improve student learning as well.

10. Why do most lists have ten items, and almost always are created in even numbers, with the possible exception of the number five?

The Problems of a "Best Practices" Student Evaluation

Pepperdine professor and division chair, Steve Rouse, uses a midterm student evaluation with his students to elicit feedback. He cautions that the instrument he uses should never be used in formal teacher evaluation, even though the device asks students about factors that have been found to correlate with student achievement and strong student evaluations of teachers. He himself knows that an individual teacher may successfully ignore any or all of the factors contained in the evaluation form. What tends to be true for teachers as a group is not necessarily true for an individual.

Here are the questions he asks his students at midterms, knowing that these behaviors may not be ones that he values for his own teaching.

The Teacher Behavior Checklist*

Instructions: Listed below are twenty-eight teacher qualities and the behaviors that define them. Please rate me on the extent to which you believe I possess these qualities and exhibit the corresponding behaviors.

a. You never exhibit the behaviors reflective of this quality.
b. You rarely exhibit the behaviors reflective of this quality.
c. You sometimes exhibit the behaviors reflective of this quality.
d. You frequently exhibit the behaviors reflective of this quality.

e. You almost always exhibit the behaviors reflective of this quality.

1. ABCDE *Accessible* (Posts office hours, gives out phone number and email information)
2. ABCDE *Approachable/Personable* (Smiles, greets students, initiates conversations, invites questions, responds respectfully to student comments)
3. ABCDE *Authoritative* (Establishes clear course rules, maintains classroom order, speaks in a loud, strong voice)
4. ABCDE *Confident* (Speaks clearly, makes eye contact, and answers questions correctly)
5. ABCDE *Creative and Interesting* (Experiments with teaching methods; uses technological devices to support and enhance lectures; uses interesting, relevant, and personal examples; not monotone)
6. ABCDE *Effective Communicator* (Speaks clearly/loudly, uses precise English; gives clear, compelling examples)
7. ABCDE *Encourages and Cares for Students* (Provides praise for good student work, helps students who need it, offers bonus points and extra credit, and knows student names)
8. ABCDE *Enthusiastic about Teaching and about Topic* (Smiles during class, prepares interesting class activities, uses gestures and expressions of emotion to emphasize important points, and arrives on time for class)
9. ABCDE *Establishes Daily and Academic Term Goals* (Prepares/follows a syllabus and has goals for each class)
10. ABCDE *Flexible/Open-Minded* (Changes calendar of course events when necessary, will meet at hours outside of office hours, pays attention to students when they state their opinions, accepts criticism from others, and allows students to do make-up work when appropriate)
11. ABCDE *Good Listener* (Doesn't interrupt students while they are talking, maintains eye contact, and asks questions about points that students are making)
12. ABCDE *Happy/Positive Attitude/Humorous* (Tells jokes and funny stories, laughs with students)
13. ABCDE *Humble* (Admits mistakes, never brags, and doesn't take credit for others' successes)
14. ABCDE *Knowledgeable about Subject Matter* (Easily answers students' questions, does not read straight from the book or notes, and uses clear and understandable examples)
15. ABCDE *Prepared* (Brings necessary materials to class, is never late for class, provides outlines of class discussion)

16. ABCDE *Presents Current Information* (Relates topic to current, real-life situations; uses recent videos, magazines, and newspapers to demonstrate points; talks about current topics; uses new or recent texts)

17. ABCDE *Professional* (Dresses nicely [neat and clean shoes, slacks, blouses, dresses, shirts, ties] and no profanity)

18. ABCDE *Promotes Class Discussion* (Asks controversial or challenging questions during class, gives points for class participation, involves students in group activities during class)

19. ABCDE *Promotes Critical Thinking/Intellectually Stimulating* (Asks thoughtful questions during class, uses essay questions on tests and quizzes, assigns homework, and holds group discussions/activities)

20. ABCDE *Provides Constructive Feedback* (Writes comments on returned work, answers students' questions, and gives advice on test taking)

21. ABCDE *Punctuality/Manages Class Time* (Arrives to class on time/early, dismisses class on time, presents relevant materials in class, leaves time for questions, keeps appointments, returns work in a timely way)

22. ABCDE *Rapport* (Makes class laugh through jokes and funny stories, initiates and maintains class discussions, knows student names, interacts with students before and after class)

23. ABCDE *Realistic Expectations of Students/Fair Testing and Grading* (Covers material to be tested during class, writes relevant test questions, does not overload students with reading, teaches at an appropriate level for the majority of students in the course, curves grades when appropriate)

24. ABCDE *Respectful* (Does not humiliate or embarrass students in class, is polite to students [says thank you and please, etc.], does not interrupt students while they are talking, does not talk down to students)

25. ABCDE *Sensitive and Persistent* (Makes sure students understand material before moving to new material, holds extra study sessions, repeats information when necessary, asks questions to check student understanding)

26. ABCDE *Strives to Be a Better Teacher* (Requests feedback on his/her teaching ability from students, continues learning [attends workshops, etc., on teaching], and uses new teaching methods)

27. ABCDE *Technologically Competent* (Knows how to use a computer, knows how to use email with students, knows how to use overheads during class, has a web page for classes)

28. ABCDE *Understanding* (Accepts legitimate excuses for missing class or coursework, is available before/after class to answer questions, does not lose temper at students, takes extra time to discuss difficult concepts)

* The Teacher Behavior Checklist was developed by William Buskist and Jared Keeley at Auburn University. Permission has been given to use and revise this checklist for personal use.

■■■

For the great teacher each of these potential teaching variables is very problematic. The enormous problem with this list is that at least one of the thirty-two great teachers of this study violates the standard expected by this questionnaire, and in ways that thus invalidate it as an objective standard for great teaching. The twenty-eight questions above are like "best practices"; they may work generally, but that does not guarantee that they will work particularly for individual teachers.

Take for example #17, professional dress. If a teacher wants good student evaluations, the default position would be to "dress up" or perhaps don a lab coat. But as Emerson asks, Who is the man who could teach Shakespeare?, the great teacher is more likely, consciously or unconsciously, to go against the dress tendencies and norms of the particular teaching staff. Intuitively the great teacher uses even dress to signal to students something different, something special is expected to occur.

If you are satisfied with "good" and want to play it safe, by all means adapt to each of those twenty-eight expectations. Your overall student evaluation score may be at stake. However, great teachers violate such norms at will, with purpose and to even greater success.

A footnote: Should the great teacher defy an expectation like "professional dress" norms and be required to use a student evaluation form like the one Steve Rouse uses, know that the great teacher will likely get the highest mark regardless. Students make a holistic judgment about the quality of the teacher, and after that, whatever the subsequent questions, they all tend to intercorrelate with that overall judgment.

This study argues that great teaching requires a different set of characteristics than those associated with good teaching. Great teaching by definition exceeds the norms. The Teacher Behavior Checklist below has been based on characteristics that have been found by the research to associate with student learning, and yet not one of these characteristics sets an inviolable standard for the great teacher. Quite the contrary. Great teachers take exception to any thought that teacher characteristics might be prescribed, because a great teacher quite likely violates the expectation, and does so to achieve great teaching.

1. *Accessible* (Posts office hours, gives out phone number and email information).

   Accessibility is a relative term. Posted office hours for professors are mostly useless for the great teacher because the great teacher's students will need to see her/him in a much more timely fashion than during posted hours. One of the great teachers from the acknowledgments section observes privately that if the teacher is doing his/her job in the classroom, the students for the most part will not need to see him. With certain students, especially "spoiled children," overaccessibility may send the wrong message about the importance of the teacher and the teacher's time.

   Are teachers like Rafe Esquith, Jaime Escalante, and Elliot Eisner to be rated less accessible because they are asked to visit other schools so often? Some of the great teachers do not post office hours, some do not give out their phone numbers, and some do not use email. In answering this question the student evaluator may answer on the basis of was that teacher there the one time the student went looking for her/him, and so it is not the kind of question that should be in a list of expected or required teacher characteristics should this instrument be used to evaluate a great teacher. It should be added, however, that a low score on any one of the items from the checklist is strong evidence of some sort of student dissatisfaction that needs the non–great teacher's attention.

2. *Approachable/Personable* (Smiles, greets students, initiates conversations, invites questions, responds respectfully to student comments)

   While presumably being approachable and personable are positive human characteristics, the great teacher has a greater concern for establishing the challenge that the teacher and course expects to make. Friendliness is something to be earned over time. Usually to their surprise once they have risen to the challenge, students find the very demanding teacher with such high expectations also happens to be approachable and personable.

3. *Authoritative* (Establishes clear course rules, maintains classroom order, speaks in a loud, strong voice)

   Elsewhere in this study five forms of authority are discussed, and great teachers use each of those forms as necessary in response to given students and classes. But with the possible exception of the KIPP teachers, great teachers do not establish clear course rules. Life in the classroom is too complex for a simple set of rules. The golden rule and the American Constitution would be more appropriate alternatives. Great teachers create a community in which students are expected to look out for one another, and while there may be expectations about such things as assignment due dates, the emphasis is on responsibility and community rather than keeping track of rule infractions and inflicting set penalties.

While most of the core list of great teachers maintains what might be perceived as orderly classrooms, some great teachers foment the kind of classroom responses that a bit of disorder can also be prized. And a loud, strong voice? Great teachers speaking with integrity speak with whatever pitch and timbre they choose. Escalante was loud; Jimenez was quiet. Great teachers are not likely to trust the administrators in authority for recognizing how well they wield power, since most of the ways are set up early and seldom are seen by an observer thereafter.

The connotations of "authoritative" may also be problematic for students trying to evaluate this quality in a great teacher, because the term can suggest being "authoritarian," and great teachers are most anxious to have their students work from an internal locus of control as much as possible. While the characteristic may work for most teachers in a way that leads to student achievement, the characteristic as described does not communicate what the great teacher is about.

4. *Confident* (Speaks clearly, makes eye contact, and answers questions correctly)

Certainly great teachers have confidence, but note that this is certainly not one of the distinguishing qualities of a great teacher, not because they do not have it, but because it is so assumed. Certainly all thirty-two great teachers of this study's core group speak clearly and make eye contact, and presumably answer questions correctly, but the key to great teachers' confidence is their willingness to experiment, to take risks, to persevere in the face of their own doubts, to pursue questions to which they do not have the answers.

Students probably think of these teachers as confident, but the budding great teacher might realize that the great teachers are more acutely aware of the ways in which they lack confidence. The chapter 3 factors that identify ways in which great teachers became that way might include an item: "Has their lack of confidence under some control."

5. *Creative and Interesting* (Experiments with teaching methods; uses technological devices to support and enhance lectures; uses interesting, relevant, and personal examples; not monotone)

David Tyack experimented with teaching methods a lot more than John Daly did, and Joe Cattarin managed his great teaching relying on lecture. Many of these great teachers eschewed technology. Certainly all of them were interesting, but it might be said that those like Eisner made themselves interesting, while those like Tyack put a greater emphasis on bringing out what was most interesting in the students. As before, while being creative and interesting are good human qualities, if they are not particularly characteristic of all the great teachers they cannot be "required" expectations. The argument here is that if a less effective teacher might get a higher score on this characteristic than a great teacher, the characteristic needs to be disregarded in the formal assessment and evaluation of the great teacher.

6. *Effective Communicator* (Speaks clearly/loudly, uses precise English; gives clear, compelling examples)

Because communication involves at least two people, evaluating only one on the basis of clarity and precision seems ill advised. Not all of the core group of great teachers spoke clearly or loudly or used precise English. Professor David Holmes, a great teacher cited in the acknowledgments, makes great use of switching back and forth between slang and formal English; Escalante was known to take great liberties with English; Lewis Owen would speak occasionally in both Old and Middle English as if students should understand him. Larry Giacomino, Elizabeth Cohen, Arturo Pacheco, and others placed such an emphasis on their students' communication skills that their own might be undervalued on such an evaluation as this one.

7. *Encourages and Cares for Students* (Provides praise for good student work, helps students who need it, offers bonus points and extra credit, and knows student names)

Even something as seemingly obvious as "provides praise for good student work" is not always a good idea per se. Quite possibly "spoiled children" need to learn to work harder before given praise. Students who can do better than good work may need to find that their good work is not acceptable. One of the young, great teachers from the acknowledgments section, now a professor, was once told in college that "if he wasn't going to do papers any better than the one he had turned in, not to do any more papers for that class." That lack of encouragement was apparently what that student needed to hear at the time.

Caring comes in quite different packages. Perhaps none of the thirty-two core group of great teachers offered bonus points or extra credit, but neither did they have rigid point systems for grading students. Jaime Escalante may be the only teacher on the list who did not know all of his students' names, but if a great teacher can be great without meeting this expectation, then, again, the argument here is that it cannot be a set expectation for comparing one teacher to another.

Indeed, to repeat, Steve Rouse, who uses this device as a midterm student evaluation, finds this instrument extremely valuable, but only for his own use. The absolute key is in recognizing that students may have these expectations, and the students' answers may suggest to the discerning teacher what adjustments and clarifications may be needed to match what the teacher values to what the students value.

As a formative evaluation, where the results are not seen in any way as prescriptive, this student evaluation can be very effective. But the enormous worry, especially among great teachers, is that in the wrong hands, administrators will unilaterally value these apparent "best practices" and think that these are the preferred standards for all teachers. Great teachers need to be recognized for doing things quite differently and in ways in which our small group of thirty-two great teachers violate every one of the list's behaviors.

8. *Enthusiastic about Teaching and about Topic* (Smiles during class, prepares interesting class activities, uses gestures and expressions of emotion to emphasize important points, and arrives on time for class)

Two compliments most often given to teachers with low student evaluations were that they were "knowledgeable" and "enthusiastic." That is not a misprint—these are the compliments for the lowest ranked teachers. What matters is whether the teachers have found a way to make students knowledgeable and enthusiastic about the subject. The specific descriptions of behaviors associated with this characteristic are also problematic.

John Daly rarely smiled or used gestures and expressions of emotion to emphasize important points. Anal-retentive martinets may be on time for class; great teachers are on time because they can hardly wait to get started. That was so true for one teacher that his/her classes started when everyone was there, which was often before it was scheduled to start. Students come to a holistic decision about the quality of the teacher, and then no matter what the student evaluation questions, they will tend to intercorrelate. Great teachers would undoubtedly do well on this item, but if it is what is most commonly said as the nicest thing that can be said about a poor teacher, what sort of value does it have on the summative evaluation of a great teacher?

9. *Establishes Daily and Academic Term Goals* (Prepares/follows a syllabus and has goals for each class)

Educational research has found that overpreparation makes for inauthentic teaching. Overprepared teachers tend to try to force feed the lesson instead of responding to the students' responses. Great teachers have goals, and probably a syllabus, but recognizing their class as a lab, it is just as important when raising the issue of daily and term goals and a syllabus to avoid what happens when the detail of the syllabus is mistaken as a sign of effective teaching. Also, too often goals are limited to objectives that have the limitations of 1) emphasizing what is most easily recognized and written; 2) emphasizing lower levels of cognition; 3) neglecting the interrelationships of the most important objectives; and 4) failing to set themselves in the context of the greater purposes of an education.

Great teachers know what they have in mind for students so well that even if the particular class topic is as specific as teaching about plot, or occasions versus causes, or entropy, or isosceles triangles, the great teacher will be open to recognize "teachable moments" that might be about study skills, the relationship of the topic to the subject as a whole, and how it contributes to the meaning of life. The "time on task" research tends to emphasize low levels of learning; Decker Walker found that students do well on tests that measure what they were taught. The great teacher is nervous that the emphasis on daily goals may be at the neglect of other vital issues and may turn out to be better handled at another time during the class.

10. *Flexible/Open-Minded* (Changes calendar of course events when necessary, will meet at hours outside of office hours, pays attention to students when they state their opinions, accepts criticism from others, and allows students to do make-up work when appropriate)

Emerson says that the self-reliant person is immune to criticism, while Virginia Woolf maintains that it is the exceptional person who takes particular offense at criticism. Just as paradox can be thought of as a way of understanding wisdom, both Emerson and Woolf are correct as far as the great teacher goes. As mentioned elsewhere, famous Georgetown basketball coach John Thompson elicited the observation that "normal folk questioned where and how he got so sure."

Great teachers tend to have spent inordinate amounts of time thinking about their choices, so while in fact they are flexible and open-minded, they may not appear so since they are impatient with uninformed opinions and criticisms. Thus they may very well be a bit testy with students who are too quick to espouse an opinion without having thought first; edgy with the student who has too easy an excuse with regard to make-up work; impatient with a student who has missed an earlier appointment without probable cause and without notifying the teacher. Great teachers are not easy pushovers, so a quality like being flexible and open-minded may not be the qualities most easily recognized in the great teacher.

11. *Good Listener* (Doesn't interrupt students while they are talking, maintains eye contact, and asks questions about points that students are making)

Even great teachers are often better at either listening or speaking, and the difference tends to make for an invidious comparison. The great discussant often anticipates extremely well, and they may short-circuit the long student question to get more quickly at what the class as a whole wants to know. Yes, they may interrupt the student to keep the conversation flowing. The great teacher tends to anticipate well, so in fact the listening is usually quite good, and he or she is equally adept at pursuing a question with a student to get at clarifying the student's question to the student.

Most of the core group of great teachers were good listeners in terms of quickly grasping what was behind a student question, but if fact be told, they are also adept at cutting off the long-winded student and keeping the discussion flowing, a talent well appreciated by classes as a whole, and done well enough so that the individual student was not resentful.

12. *Happy/Positive Attitude/Humorous* (Tells jokes and funny stories, laughs with students)

Of all the great teachers in history none may have written funnier stories than teacher/author Jim Herndon. Jaime Escalante and Gene Bream are both reported to have been extremely humorous. Certainly students prize this characteristic. However, this investigation did not find telling jokes, funny stories, or laughing with students to be a major characteristic of all the thirty-two teachers on our list. Thus it cannot be required as a characteristic for the true evaluation of a great teacher. But that humor is both associated with student learning and a characteristic that is not inconsistent with great teaching seems evident.

13. *Humble* (Admits mistakes, never brags, and doesn't take credit for others' successes)

If a great teacher promotes one of his/her students for a major award, that support is also inherently somewhat self-serving, since the teacher may seem to be associated with the results. Great teachers are often, and probably always, thought of as arrogant by some, especially those who are jealous or who think that the great teachers are somehow pressuring them to work harder as well. As described elsewhere in this study, great teachers tend to speak up only about topics in which they are well versed, and they refrain from doing more than asking questions in areas where they are not. That can create a public image of arrogance because only the confidence is made public. When great teachers write about themselves, whether Ashton-Warner, Herndon, Inchausti, Esquith, or others, they tend to dwell on their many shortcomings, failures, and insecurities.

In the final analysis great teachers may be the ones most likely to meet Aristotle's understanding of the golden mean—neither rashly arrogant, nor timidly humble, just honest about what they likely can and cannot do. However, because they are trying to drive students to exceed their own expectations, many great teachers will tend to say outrageous things, perhaps like "this probably will be the best class you ever take, and I should be your favorite teacher since I undoubtedly like you better than any of your others did." Such is not a lack of humility; and its hyperbole is well intended. But do not evaluate great teachers on a characteristic like humility, because some students will want to credit the great teacher with any and all virtues but other students will think that the teacher is too good to be called humble.

14. *Knowledgeable about Subject Matter* (Easily answers students' questions, does not read straight from the book or notes, and uses clear and understandable examples)

As stated about enthusiasm above, the two bones most commonly thrown to the least effective teacher is that at least she or he was enthusiastic and knowledgeable. Even the most seriously misplaced teacher in terms of subject matter will know more about that subject than 99 percent of the students will ever want to know. What usually makes the students think that this is a teacher who best knows his/her subject matter is the ability to see how the subject relates to other knowledge.

As with the question on enthusiasm, if this is not a question that tends to distinguish the qualities of great teaching, it needs to be handled very discreetly. David Tyack is recognized as one of the country's most knowledgeable about the history of education. Elliot Eisner's field has been known historically as "general curriculum." Tyack's field is more clearly defined, but that does not mean that he should automatically receive a higher teaching evaluation than Eisner.

15. *Prepared* (Brings necessary materials to class, is never late for class, provides outlines of class discussion)

Cohen was the only one from the list of great teachers who often provided students with outlines of the course discussions. Great teachers would never likely let on that they forgot to bring something to class, so who would know? Great teachers know that they have been preparing their whole lives for the next moment and that overpreparation does not improve teaching. But the great teachers of this list are thought to be prepared to take on the next class because they have been looking forward to the engagement. The description of prepared behavior above trivializes what preparation includes for great teachers.

16. *Presents Current Information* (Relates topic to current, real-life situations; uses recent videos, magazines, and newspapers to demonstrate points; talks about current topics; uses new or recent texts)

Gene Bream may be the greatest of the greatest at this. But what were Jaime Escalante and Ben Jimenez going to do with this expectation for Advanced Placement Calculus? Such a question favors some subjects over others, thus while an especially useful question for a social studies course, it has less relevance in other subjects, and thus it privileges one kind of teaching over another. Again, this is a great item for a psychology teacher like Steve Rouse, who also knows how to read the results, keeping in mind his intentions versus possible students' expectations. By using it as a formative evaluation, he can make some changes or help students to realize why he emphasizes what he emphasizes. But items like this cannot be used in a school's qualitative evaluations of teachers because it is unfair in the way it privileges some subjects over others.

17. *Professional* (Dresses nicely [neat and clean shoes, slacks, blouses, dresses, shirts, ties] and no profanity)

Joe Cattarin wore a coat and tie to teach at Half Moon Bay High School. He was the only teacher who wore a coat and tie, thus his attire helped him set up the expectation among students that something different and something special was going to happen in his classes. But it would be ludicrous for his dress to set the standards for great teachers. David Holmes would occasionally wear a Lakers jersey; Caleb Clanton almost always wears sandals. Alice Coleman wore her pearls. Lewis Owen his English tweeds. Peter Tracey his Norfolk jacket. John Daly had his Ivy League ties. Paul Beck wore a flat top.

Steve Rouse gives this questionnaire to his own students, knowing that he does not necessarily plan to wear a coat and tie to teach. Great teachers tend to find a look that is unique enough in its school setting to signal something special is expected to occur. A question like this should never be used for a school's evaluation of teachers. But some teachers may find it useful in a midterm evaluation because it is one area for which students have expectations that need not be ignored just because it is otherwise inane.

18. *Promotes Class Discussion* (Asks controversial or challenging questions during class, gives points for class participation, involves students in group activities during class)

This is another one of those items that tends to privilege some subjects over others, but even Beck's PE classes consistently elicited locker-room discussions about what was fair within competition, Escalante's math classes about social issues, and Giacomino's science classes about ecology. The item must not be used to privilege the subjects where this happens the most, but it is a worthy goal of any course.

But the issue of "points" for discussion needs to be rejected entirely. For example, a student received a "B" in a high school language course because she had less participation points. The teacher gives these points in terms of responses to her recitation questions. What about the student who raised her hand every time but was called on less often? That sort of thing happens far too often with participation points. They tend to measure the teacher's preferences, not the students' performances. Also, points tend to elicit a competition for a teacher's attention rather than actually rewarding students for having something smart and well considered to contribute to class. The likelihood of a teacher accurately grading true contributions to discussion are nil unless a second teacher is able to do the judging while the first teacher leads the discussion.

19. *Promotes Critical Thinking/Intellectually Stimulating* (Asks thoughtful questions during class, uses essay questions on tests and quizzes, assigns homework, and holds group discussions/activities)

    None of these great teachers were likely to use quizzes. Quizzes tend to emphasize trivial knowledge and teach the students to hate the subject matter. (See the section on students asking ten questions in the section on assessment for an alternative.) Yet still again, this question tends to privilege subjects more given to discussion, yet all great teachers take every opportunity to promote critical thinking and discussion. Recent research on students learning to ask their own quality questions suggests that it is at least as important for students to learn to ask quality questions as for teachers to ask them.

20. *Provides Constructive Feedback* (Writes comments on returned work, answers students' questions, and gives advice on test taking)

    Great teachers give constructive feedback about the coursework, about the student's basic academic skills, and about potential educational aspirations. Most of the great teachers from the core list were often thought of by students to have written as many words on their papers as the students had written themselves. Such detailed responses are helpful in the particular, they verify the seriousness of the work, and they help motivate the class that knows that the great teacher is working even harder than the student.

21. *Punctuality/Manages Class Time* (Arrives to class on time/early, dismisses class on time, presents relevant materials in class, leaves time for questions, keeps appointments, returns work in a timely way)

    Great teachers show respect for their students by honoring the class's start and stop times and honoring scheduled breaks. Great teachers are conscientious across the board, especially about appointments (and expecting students to keep them). They return students' work in a timely way so that the feedback is meaningful. This characteristic, however, does not necessarily sort out the great teachers from other teachers, and the emphasis on punctuality might be achieved by a Felix Unger as well as a great teacher.

The underlying quality to punctuality is dedication, and the commitment that all the identified great teachers have in setting high expectations, using their class as a lab, and creating a sense of community symbolically starts with attention to such important matters as punctuality and use of class time. All thirty-two teachers certainly met this characteristic.

22. *Rapport* (Makes class laugh through jokes and funny stories, initiates and maintains class discussions, knows student names, interacts with students before and after class)

   Humor is certainly a way of establishing and maintaining rapport with students, but not the only way. Daly's concern for students' college aspirations, Coleman's for students' writing skills, Beck's for students' responsible behavior, Owen's for students' graduate school aspirations, others' for what books students were reading, what films they were seeing, what places they had visited are all alternative topics that build rapport. Even when Escalante could not remember names he had a sense of each student. The imperative to the interaction for the great teacher is that it is genuine. Perhaps the term *rapport* suggests genuineness, but this item would do better to go beyond jokes and names to establish how great teachers use rapport as a part of building a sense of community.

23. *Realistic Expectations of Students/Fair Testing and Grading* (Covers material to be tested during class, writes relevant test questions, does not overload students with reading, teaches at an appropriate level for the majority of students in the course, curves grades when appropriate)

   The problem for the great teacher with this item is what does "realistic expectations" mean? Great teachers want to extend realistic expectations to challenge the students to realize that they can most likely exceed their current self-expectations. This item invites a student to complain too readily about a teacher's workload.

   Great teachers emphasize rigor and robustness rather than length, quantity, and busy work. Great teachers will use any number of grading systems, including curves, dropping an exam, giving more weight to certain tests, and recognizing that eventually the teacher is the true measure, not just any points they may have assigned in an attempt to be more fair. Too many subject-matter specialist-type teachers give tests that try to catch students in what they did not learn. Such tests can often trivialize the subject's most important knowledge as it finds the peculiar questions that only the "A" students might answer.

   As a rule great teachers will see that 60 percent of the exam will cover what everyone surely learned, and with the remaining 40 percent they try to sort out the higher grades. Such testing communicates to the entire class that the entire class is learning. Great teachers will not compromise their standards for the grade of "A," but they have more than one way students might earn "Cs" and "Bs."

24. *Respectful* (Does not humiliate or embarrass students in class, is polite to students [says thank you and please, etc.], does not interrupt students while they are talking, does not talk down to students)

Great teachers respect their students, and not superficially so. They establish the right to tell students the truth as candidly as possible. They establish trust in such a way that students' work can be criticized in class such that it is not taken personally, and it is seen by one and all to be helpful feedback toward the excellence that the teacher knows that they all can achieve.

Great teachers often (with the students' permission) share student work with the class. Seeing what was good and could have been better about a classmate's work can be extremely helpful, as long as the students all know that the criticism is to lead to better work and higher grades. A great teacher works very hard to get the students to be able to respond well to constructive criticism and that such criticism is to be prized and not feared.

25. *Sensitive and Persistent* (Makes sure students understand material before moving to new material, holds extra study sessions, repeats information when necessary, asks questions to check student understanding)

Levin and Feinberg were not thought to be so particularly sensitive with their students so much as committed and persistent. Using the class as a lab, great teachers are especially dedicated to following the progress of each and every student. However, great teachers also want the individual student, and then the individual student in conjunction with their peers, to pursue problems with due diligence before leaning on the teacher for extra help.

26. *Strives to Be a Better Teacher* (Requests feedback on his/her teaching ability from students, continues learning [attends workshops, etc., on teaching], and uses new teaching methods)

Great teachers rely primarily upon themselves. They tend to trust their own reading of a situation more than most available feedback from others and other sources. Workshops tend to take more time than the payoff makes worthwhile. Great teachers are as likely to create a new way of solving a classroom problem as to borrow one. They tend not to watch others teach, because they know others' successes are not likely to translate into their own best way of doing things. Great teachers have a great nose for what will work for them and a quick eye for quickly recognizing and rejecting what is not likely to be helpful. Great teachers might quickly scan one hundred possibilities and iden-

tify the one idea, suggestion, or method that would be worth their time
to try. And young great teachers will do well to quit letting Noman tell
them otherwise—they are perspicacious and can quickly pick and
choose on the basis of what their intuition and limited experience tells
them.

27. *Technologically Competent* (Knows how to use a computer, knows
how to use email with students, knows how to use overheads during
class, has a web page for classes)

Great teachers will do what is necessary to be great. Some of the
core lists of great teachers resist technology. Probably all of the next
generation will incorporate technology. However, such an item as this
has no place in the evaluation of a great teacher because the great
teacher will know best for herself or himself.

28. *Understanding* (Accepts legitimate excuses for missing class or
coursework, is available before/after class to answer questions, does
not lose temper at students, takes extra time to discuss difficult concepts)

Nonsense. When a great teacher has established credibility and high
expectations, the teacher can seem to lose her/his temper. The key is
that students recognize that such is just. Further, the teacher makes a
distinction between reasons and excuses and helps the students make
such distinctions so that there are an absolute minimum of times when
excuses are made. Having established such high expectations, once
the student has put in the time, of course the teacher extends herself or
himself to helping the student as much as necessary.

BEYOND EXCELLENCE

How have the great teachers transcended excellence? This section hypothe-
sizes that great teachers base their work in values that transcend self. The
perspectives in this section are potentially helpful for considering some of
the ways a sense of the transcendent might be grasped.

Spranger's Values

Eduard Spranger has identified six value "vectors" that he sees as fundamental values that tend to create personal "direction" (in Gose, 2006:70–73). He
identifies:

1. The Theoretical (intellectual concern for the discovery of truth)
2. The Economic (interested in what is useful, profitable)
3. The Aesthetic (values art, form, beauty)

4. The Social (love of people)
5. The Political (interest in politics, power, influence)
6. The Religious (keenly interested in the spiritual)

Chapter 3 asserts on the basis of very little documentation that great teachers have integrity based on or within something greater than themselves. All teachers, and especially great teachers, will presumably get in touch with that personal core or enlightening ideal to sustain the demands of not only teaching but also great teaching. Such a base is undoubtedly more important than all the elements of this book, but for the most part the great teachers of this book have been rather mute about their philosophies of life.

A source for considering values that might be central and integral for a budding great teacher is Spranger's list of fundamental human values. Of this study's core great teachers, Tyack was probably grounded in the theoretical; Robert Sexton (cited in the Acknowledgments section) in the economic; Eisner in the aesthetic; Shaftel in the social; Hawkinshire in the political; Clark in the religious. Each or all may have believed in ideals, in the Forms of the Good; each or all may have been existentialists choosing their fundamental value vector. But all that is idle speculation about them. Great teachers are oriented to fomenting their students' growth and not having an undue influence on what that growth might entail. Inspiring, not proselytizing. The surmise: Great teachers' strength is well founded in values beyond themselves.

The Counterhero

Why is it that the best teachers seem to have conflict with "administration"? Many of the ins and outs of the "counterhero" role are assumed by at least a great many great teachers. The long, working definition below is offered because it may be a warning to some who will not choose to be a great teacher and because it might help clarify the different ideals of those practicing the role on behalf of their great teaching. The counterhero role fits as a prototype for at least many great teachers.

A Working Definition of the Counterhero (adapted from Gose, 1999:180–84)

Maureen Fries (*Popular Arthurian Traditions*) defines a "counterhero" as someone who "possesses the hero's superior power of action without possessing his or her adherence to the dominant culture or capability of renewing its values."

An expanded, working definition of counterhero includes all of the following characteristics: a "counterhero" a) does not always have to prevail; b) does not have to always assert a macho presence; c) does not always need to win; d) can defer to others; e) can stand up to traditional authority, traditional ways of doing things, and traditional values while offering alternative values that seem more salient. And she or he does all of this while still being heroic and while asserting a place within the mainstream, whether it is fully appreciated by others or not.

In general: The counterhero is not a traditional hero but still has a role in the mainstream. The counterhero often provides an "alternative voice" within the mainstream. The counterhero has the strengths of the traditional hero but uses those strengths toward different ends. The counterhero challenges the status quo by personifying values that undercut the values of the dominant culture. This creates conflict with and in the dominant culture such that the counterhero is as likely to be at odds with the traditional powers as with the villains.

The counterhero has a different set of personal characteristics from that of the traditional hero. The counterhero:

- is only reluctantly the hero
- deems it okay to be conflicted and/or flawed but must work regardless toward the right things
- is intelligent, but tends to come reluctantly to a realization of what needs to be done
- makes a distinction between righteousness and self-righteousness
- may at times be thought of as heroic by others but is not trying to be a role model per se
- knows that no good deed goes unpunished

The counterhero has a different orientation toward others than that of the traditional hero. The counterhero:

- usually is more of an informal rather than formal leader within a group (or the formal leader of a group trying to change things within the system)
- most often tries to use the system to fix the system, usually fighting inside rather than outside the system
- is more likely a populist, democratic in orientations, rather than a staunch individualist (which does not mean she or he will not take a strong position on an issue)
- is more reactionary than revolutionary in that action is more likely to come from a realization that "well, that isn't right"
- may intentionally or inadvertently speak for others, but tends to stand alone instead of democratically working with others to establish consensus

The counterhero is reactionary in that she or he is reacting to the values of the dominant culture, not necessarily by rejecting those values entirely, but in emphasizing a counter set of values.

Counter values to an emphasis on success:

- does not always have to prevail, win, or succeed
- is more likely to see a moral victory in defeat
- is more likely to go ahead and take part in a losing cause
- accepts that one cannot win every battle

Counter values to an emphasis on competition:

- has a more conspicuous regard for the feelings of others
- has a greater emphasis on the competition of ideas than on interpersonal competition
- tends to take the side of the underdog
- is more likely to seek advice
- can defer to others (without it being a challenge to confidence or efficacy)
- does not have to assert a macho presence
- is reluctantly willful (in insisting on what is perceived to be right)

Counter values to an emphasis on striving:

- has a sense of humor
- can take self less seriously
- is more likely to stop and smell the roses
- emphasizes living in the present more than preparing for the future

Counter values to materialism:

- places a greater emphasis on friendships and relationships than things
- puts a greater emphasis on relationships and has a noted regard for the other sex
- appreciates the small things with no great appetite for expensive worldly goods

Counter values to external conformity:

- can suggest alternative ways of doing things
- has a personal rather than external standard of success
- is likely to raise questions of authority
- will try to hold traditional authorities responsible regardless of the probable payoff or cost to popularity

- is quite probably outspoken and even subversive
- is not an outlaw, but walks to the beat of a different drummer
- inevitably is a challenge to the status quo
- doesn't go along with things just to go along with things
- is nonconforming, but in the mainstream
- is less tolerant of bureaucracy
- is oriented toward creative problem solving
- has significant ability and confidence in the ability to take a position different from the mainstream

Values of the counterhero:

- a more conspicuous regard for the feelings of others than the traditional hero
- a noted regard for the other sex
- more emphasis on the competition of ideas than on interpersonal competition
- seemingly less emphasis on materialism
- personal rather than external standards of success
- tends to take the side of the underdog
- more likely to seek advice
- willingness to change (it's not a badge of honor to insist on how one's always done things)

Relation to others (including authority):

- can defer to others (without it being a challenge to their self-concept)
- can suggest alternative ways of doing things
- usually more of an informal than formal leader within the group (or the formal leader of a group trying to change things but still within the system)
- most often tries to use the system to fix the system, usually by fighting inside rather than outside of the system
- more likely a populist, democratic in orientation, rather than a staunch individualist (which does not mean she or he will not take a strong position on an issue)
- likely to raise questions, especially of authority
- will try to hold traditional authorities responsible regardless of the obvious payoff or cost to popularity
- more reactionary than revolutionary in that action is more likely to come from a realization of "well, that isn't right"
- quite probably at times outspoken and even subversive

- a counterhero may advertently or inadvertently speak for others, but tends to stand alone instead of democratically working with others to establish consensus

This working definition of the counterhero fleshes out how at least some of the great teachers work out that certain kind of insubordination that tends to be a characteristic of great teaching.

Existential Dilemmas

Teachers face sixteen existential dilemmas (as identified by Ann and Harold Berlak, 1981:135–65), or why a foolish consistency is the hobgoblin of little minds.

1. whole person versus person as student
2. teacher versus student control of time
3. teacher versus student control of operations
4. teacher versus student control of standards
5. personal versus public knowledge
6. knowledge as content versus knowledge as process
7. knowledge as given versus knowledge as problematic
8. intrinsic versus extrinsic motivation
9. learning is holistic versus learning is molecular
10. student is unique versus student has shared characteristics
11. learning is social versus learning is individual
12. student as person versus student as client
13. childhood is continuous versus childhood is unique
14. equal allocation of resources versus differential allocation
15. equal justice under the law versus ad hoc application of the rules
16. common culture versus subgroup consciousness

Great teachers tend to suffer great angst. They know full well that certain choices mitigate against other ones. With Emerson they know that consistency is the hobgoblin of little minds, but also that inconsistency has its own set of problems. The Berlaks' (1981) list of existential teaching dilemmas above does not help a great teacher resolve any of them, but it does help with perspective and by clarifying the reasons for the stress and sleepless nights.

The answer to each of the dilemmas is that "it depends." Depends upon the teacher's history with that student and with the class as a whole. Depends upon a dynamic tension between two compelling alternatives. Sometimes it matters what is happening with a student outside of class, how teachers want to use some of the class time, whether students do or do not have to do the homework, what the students thought of their own performance, what they want to write about from personal experience in the subject, whether teachers will give an "objective test" on the material, or a project, or a research assignment, and whether students choose to do it or the teacher insisted.

Sometimes it matters whether gerunds or loving to read is more important, whether maturity is or is not a quality of the student writing, whether the students do seat work or group work, whether that extracurricular event matters or is superfluous, whether the moment is enjoyed or used to prepare for a standardized test for future opportunities, whether some students get to go on the field trip and some do not, whether only football players are allowed to make up an exam, or whether students work in groups with friends or randomly assigned groups.

Berlak and Berlak have recognized that teachers might seem to be inconsistent in how they handle what seem to be examples of the very same problem. The reason for that apparent inconsistency is that the teacher makes "existential" decisions based on the history that teacher has had with the individual and with the class. Necessarily, in the terms of these sixteen dilemmas, teachers experience dynamic tension from each side of the issue and try to maintain a balance between the internal conflicting demands. Sometimes the teacher will come down on one side; other times the other.

1. Great teachers tend to honor the student more as a whole person than simply as a student. This is relative in that teaching takes an enormous amount of time, leaving only a limited remaining amount to find out about a student's family, or background, or interests, or school aspirations, but great teachers are open to the students beyond their role as students.
2. Great teachers share control of time more with students than other teachers, especially because what happens in class becomes dependent upon what transpires in the interaction between the teacher and students.
3. If the great teacher assigned students to make a cognitive map but a student turned in a painting or a drawing that worked as well or better than the maps, students deserve some trust for influencing operations.
4. A great teacher expects students to develop their own standards, and they communicate that in the long term such personal standards should prove more important than those set by the teacher. They communicate to the student that basketball player Michael Jordan was cut by his high school coach in eleventh grade, so mistakes are made. ("Prove me wrong.") They have criterion-referenced assignments in which students determine what was good enough. But a great teacher must always tell the truth as best she or he understands it about the most important academic assignments that are the best indicators of the student's future opportunities.

5. At the start of each unit great teacher Gene Bream asks his students to bring in any resources that they might have that would contribute. He matches those personal contributions with the official material covered in the text. Both are well regarded.

6. Supposedly students should know what gerunds are and whether Leif Erickson discovered America, but also how to find new information, write an argument, and how to read discerningly.

7. Great teachers are much more likely to treat knowledge as problematic, especially at the higher levels. Hawkinshire, Traugott, Shaftel, Tyack, and others all were more concerned with their students creating new knowledge than regurgitating any predigested facts.

8. While at least at first some students may work to please their great teachers, great teachers are having none of that. Such motivation hampers the development of students' intrinsic motivation and internal locus of control. At the beginning, and as a short-term measure, great teachers may hold out the carrot, but great teachers, fueled by their own internal fires, want the same self-motivation for their students.

9. Great teachers consistently make the connections between molecular aspects of their own subject with the larger subject issues and how the larger subject issues serve "knowledge as one." Daly related history to current politics. Eisner related education to high culture. Pacheco reveled in cultural pluralism. Shaftel taught role-playing for social values. Great teachers are big-picture thinkers and participants.

10. Great teachers compared to other teachers revel in the uniqueness of each student, but because classes tend to have students of the approximate same age, a great teacher learns to cope with factors like most first-year students in college never have enough sleep and that that impact on class is not personal nor unique. The frequently tardy student responded to the teacher's expectations that she be on time: "but this is the only class where I try to be on time."

11. The research shows that peer-assisted instruction works well, that what the student does is as important as what the teacher does, so many if not most great teachers create opportunities for students to work together. Final exams, however, are virtually always individual affairs.

12. A great teacher will recommend a student for a job, for a school, for a program. But is this a student the teacher will find a job for, ask to babysit, share a non-school-related book? As clients students warrant letters of recommendation from their teachers; as persons the teacher might on occasion intervene in a more personal way on a student's behalf.

13. Sometimes students have to prepare for their futures, and sometimes the co-curriculum is as or more important. Great teachers recognize this. Sometimes students simply must study for the next standardized exam. Other times they may suggest a class party. As Charles Dickens writes, at times, the people must be amused.

14. Great teachers consciously or intuitively realize how important "justice" is on a day-to-day basis in a classroom, that in cases of rectifactory justice, everyone must be treated the same, but with distributive justice advantages must be due or earned. Great teachers help students understand a differential allocation of resources; for example, for special education students to ensure them a more equitable opportunity for an equal education. Great teachers approve of a similar number of opportunities for females to play sports as males. They can explain, whether they approve or not, that football programs are excluded from the equal distribution formulae because they sometimes generate revenue that supports other sports.

15. Did the special education student who was the first person caught during an epidemic of cherry bombs in the school garbage cans really warrant the two-week suspension? Especially when it was well known that a football star put him up to it? The otherwise hard-nosed vice principal commuted the sentence to a one-week suspension and privately rued having given any suspension at all.

16. This issue often comes up with regard to hazing. Although hazing is against the law, seniors often feel obliged to induct a group of new students. School leaders hope fervently that any such induction will fall short of hazing because said seniors will recognize that all the students share a common culture. Great teachers tend to respect all of a student's intentions and commitments, but they work to get them to think primarily as world citizens.

To say that there are no easy answers to the above dilemmas is facile. Great teachers respect the necessary dynamic tension, and then still lose sleep because they worry they tilted the balance the wrong way.

Bottom Lines

Finding your and your students' bottom lines (for example, not everyone needs to earn a five on Advanced Placement Calculus) is discussed next.

Finding a student's bottom line (an adaptation of Gose, 2005) describes a method for finding common ground between the teacher and student. This is a technique that can be helpful in counseling and motivating students in clarifying and achieving their academic goals.

While challenging students to do their best work, great teachers also, often intuitively, know how to find a student's "bottom line." Finding a student's bottom line, the base on which s/he will make fundamental decisions, is critical for appropriately motivating that student, and especially for helping the student who might prefer actually to elevate that bottom line. This is such an important skill that it might well be included in all teacher preparation programs.

Symbolically grades are often indicators of a student's "bottom line." The student who wants to qualify for admission to the University of California truly needs to be working for an "A." That student also needs to develop the knowledge and skills for success at the University of California. A teacher can promote high levels of performance by setting rigorous standards for an "A" and helping a student achieve those standards. But those standards might not be all that attractive to the student who is not trying to finish at the top of the class or get into a prestigious university.

At the other end of the spectrum, not every student necessarily cares whether she or he passes a class. A very bright student was determined to punish his parents by flunking all of his classes. It was a conscious and for him nondebatable decision. The suggestion to that student that he transfer to another teacher, who might have more success motivating him, was not considered relevant. In fact, that prospect alarmed him. Despite his intent to fail he insisted that the class was in fact his favorite class. His bottom line was that he wanted to stay in the class, just not pass it. The teacher accommodated him by insisting that he co-operate, read, and participate, but that he would not be disciplined for refusing to do any assignments. Periodically the teacher would check with the student to see if he would not reconsider, but the student insisted until the end on the "F" that he "earned."

This concept of the bottom line applies to discipline as well as academics. There is a great divide, for example, between the student who has a behavioral problem but who still comes to class, and the truant who does not. The student who comes to class is getting something out of being there. She or he may be placating a parent or be rewarded by driving the teacher to distraction, but she or he at least for the moment wants to be there. This gives the teacher at least something to work with.

On the whole students will want to think that the teacher would want to keep them, individually, as a student, regardless of their interest and commitment to the class. Consequently, a part of a bottom line is that the student would usually prefer to stay in the class than to be sent elsewhere. That is something to work with. They do not necessarily have to pass to stay, but they do need to show respect, at least most of the time. Such a mutual understanding makes the student's and the teacher's bottom lines compatible.

The truant is a different problem. The truant has proven she or he does not really have to be in class. Finding what would coax that student back to class is very problematic—there needs to be a payoff each day. That requires an unusual dedication to finding something that makes the day meaningful for that student, and such a reward is usually very specific and different for different students. It includes that the academic reward is obvious and that the teacher believes in the student. This is actually a fairly high bottom line, but when met, tends to make the teacher more effective with all students.

The gamut between the grades "A" and "F" has a number of different potential "bottom" lines. The student who wants to graduate but currently is under 2.0 needs at least a "C" and preferably a "C+". Often an athlete needs a "D" or "C" in every class to stay eligible. Sometimes a student will be happy with a "D-" just so she or he does not have to repeat the class.

Very often a student will say that she or he wants a high grade while in fact will not work to earn that grade. Lots of students will settle for less. If a student is willing to settle for a "B," it will be a greater chore to convince her/him that they need to do better for some other reason; for example, like you, the teacher, to honestly think that they really could get into a good college if they would pay the price.

A student teacher demanded that his teaching assignment be changed. For many reasons such a change was probably not best for the program or for the student teacher. However, his unwillingly staying with the assignment could damage the program and perhaps his future teaching prospects, if he was forced to stay in that assignment. Fortunately, the student's and the program's bottom lines were compatible. He was told that he could be moved as long as he would not ask for a future letter of recommendation from the program. He decided to stay with his assignment, and he turned that assignment into a good one. He found that his bottom line was a bit different than he had originally thought.

In summary, for discipline, if you run a good classroom and want to keep every student in class, there will be a base level of co-operation because the student wants to stay. For grades, the rare student will prefer to fail. Most students prefer something between the "A" and the "F." There are a lot of ways to skin the proverbial cat and earn "C's", "C-'s", "D+'s", "D's", "D-'s". Something constructive that relates to the subject matter that a student can do at least barely to pass is most often preferable to abject failure and thus seems to be a good idea.

Even in the stricter, older days, two high school seniors, already admitted to excellent colleges, knew that they did not have to pass the PE class to graduate. So they refused to suit up for their physical education class. Coach Paul Beck, a wise, popular, and great teacher, offered them an alternative. The two spent the semester painting a mural of the school mascot on the gym wall. They did a great job; their work lasted for years; they passed PE; and

Mr. Beck recognized a bottom line that he and the two students could both live with. That is effective teaching and a skill student teachers would profit by learning.

A representative probe of a student's bottom line may include the following:

• Do you (the student) acknowledge that I, your teacher, want you in my class, and that I rather expect to be your favorite teacher?
• So, do you need to pass my class? If so, at how high a level? A "D-" will keep you from having to take the class again; a "C-" sounds a lot better than any "D," but you need a "C" average to graduate; a "B" won't necessarily keep you out of the University of California and should get you into a state university; are you trying to get any academic award?
• Need a particular grade to stay eligible for sports? What will keep you out of trouble at home? The critical point here is that a student may not be fully aware of his/her bottom line and may think that she or he needs/wants a grade different from what she or he truly has as a bottom line. Helping a student clarify this can be extremely helpful!

Taxonomy of Student Involvement

The student self-evaluation form below may not document what students are learning, and the most eager students may overrate their actual progress, but it does offer great evidence on whether the great teacher is making progress.

A Formative Evaluation

What # characterizes your level of engagement at the first week of this class?
_____

What # characterizes the highest level of engagement that you have reached now that we are midsemester? _____

1. Interest. Students are paying attention, albeit perhaps in a passive way. They are not sleeping, off task, or totally ignoring the topic being presented. They may be paying attention for different reasons—because they like the subject, they want to please the teacher, they're willing to give it a try, and so forth.
2. Engaging. These students are listening actively (to a presentation, for example) or participating in a discussion; they are completing work as assigned by the teacher; they are co-operating and "on task."
3. Committing. Students are "really involved with it" at this level. They are accepting responsibility for learning, may be totally "absorbed" in the content, sometimes finding it hard to move on to something different.

4. Internalizing. Crucial to long-term learning, at this level the light bulb is turning on for students; they really "get it." Students may seem excited or perplexed as their concentration is focused; they begin to see the connections between this new learning and what they already know and understand.
5. Interpreting. These students want to talk about what they're learning—they want to hear what others think; they're developing confidence in their own opinions and understandings about the topic—they're rethinking it even as they talk about it, and they are beginning to think about the implications.
6. Evaluating. Students at this level "own" the knowledge but may need to confirm it by talking about it with people who have not been engaged in learning with them—for example, at home, with peers outside the classroom, or in another classroom.

(This "Taxonomy of Personal Engagement" was developed by Norah Morgan and Juliana Saxton, *Asking Better Questions*, and summarized in Jackie Walsh's *Quality Questioning*, 124–25.)

■■■

Progress in students' self-report on the Taxonomy of Involvement is an excellent indicator of great teaching. Further indications of great teaching include: Do former students write and occasionally drop by the school to visit this teacher? For older students, are there lots of students asking for letters of recommendation? What kinds of things are said on student evaluations? Are they similar to the list included in chapter 7? What sort of things do students say about the teacher, including on Facebook? Do the comments include "challenging but fair," which are watchwords of excellent teaching? Is there a word on the street about this teacher being a worthwhile challenge? Great teachers personally engage their students, and their students evidence this in ways suggested by the taxonomy.

Chapter Five

Warnings

Great teachers do not operate in a vacuum. KIPP schools allowed Levin, Corcoran, and others to do their best work. Esquith found his place in Los Angeles, and even if part of the year it was outdoors, at least in Los Angeles the weather allowed that. And although only an aspect of his curriculum, his elementary students performing Shakespeare effectively put them on the map. Ashton-Warner did her best work with the Maori children from *Teacher*.

Paulo Freire was run out of two countries for being so successful with his literacy programs. Jaime Escalante and Ben Jimenez did their best work in calculus at Garfield High School. Verne Riggle was the mainstay of the same preschool for a generation. Gene Bream's summer Europe trips confirmed the special qualities of his year-long teaching. John Daly and Alice Coleman combined forces for a powerful two-year Advanced Placement and Honors program in both history and English. Dick Tingey found that he could teach anyone to read, and especially teenagers who had somehow previously failed to learn to read.

At least most of these teachers experienced as many dis-incentives as incentives in establishing their special programs. But that is not the same as having no support whatsoever. Each cobbled enough support to be hugely successful at least for a time. Lesser lights might have given up, but such great teachers as these were stubborn enough, long enough, to create something very special.

The stories about such teachers tend to describe the obstacles, and they will have been huge. But without a modicum of support from someone somewhere, they would not have had opportunity to conduct great teaching. While great teachers tend to be notorious for refusing to accept a "no," it is critical for them to find a baseline of support. Thus this is another cautionary tale. The great teachers not only face probable duress but also may have to pay steep dues along the way to position themselves in a situation that lets them take advantage of their many strengths. Some praise should go to those bureaucrats who have not entirely lost their original sense of idealism and do give such teachers their chance to succeed.

THE NEED FOR SOME INSTITUTIONAL SUPPORT AND A GOOD FIT OF STRENGTHS WITH OPPORTUNITY

Rafe Esquith observes repeatedly in his books on teaching that despite the lack of overall administrative support for his expansive commitment to teaching, he did need permission from his administrators, even when it was only permission to meet outside on the school grounds. Jaime Escalante did his best work at Garfield High School during the time when Henry Gradillas was his principal. Some level of administrative support, even if it is only "permission," is necessary for great teachers.

Great teachers also need at least some fit between the subject they are assigned to teach and their interests, and also other factors like a fitting class size. While a brilliant lecturer, Lewis Owen was much more likely to motivate his students to pursue graduate education in the context of his seminar size classes. Robert Nisbet (in Epstein, 1981:72) writes about the great teacher "Teggart of Berkeley" that his "light (was) brighter before several hundred." Minimally an administrator must be willing to match the teacher with a suitable subject and class size.

FAILURE DOES NOT GO AWAY; IN FACT, YOU BECOME MORE ACUTELY AWARE OF IT

Any teacher who might seek to be great so that s/he might experience less failure will not find such easement of the pain in the commitment to greatness. Failure does not go away; in fact, great teachers become more acutely aware of it because in raising their own levels of expectation, they invite even more events that do not meet their threshold for success. Rafe Esquith (2003:77) observes in *There Are No Short Cuts* that "every teacher has his share of disappointments, hurt, and even pain. If you care a lot, all of those aches are magnified."

Great teachers believe, rightly or wrongly, that all of their students are redeemable, thus reachable, with the right approach. Great teachers also know that this has never been found to be actually true, but only in acting as if it is true do they maximize the probabilities of reaching as many students as possible. And they also realize that some of their lessons may mature later in a student's life.

The downside of optimism? Overoptimism. As some of Rafe Esquith's (2003:89) own students had to tell him (remember it is not only the teacher-students but also the students-teacher who are engaged in the mutual learning enterprise) what he was reluctant to see for himself. "Lots of kids use you, Mr. Esquith. You just don't see it. You love them so much you don't see them clearly. You don't even know who some of your best students are." All great teachers need not have the openness of heart of an Esquith, but this is the type of warning that great teachers heed.

Thus the constant, even for the great teachers, is failure. As Esquith observes in *Teach Like Your Hair's on Fire* (2007:ix–x): "Like all real teachers, I fail constantly . . . I lie awake in the early morning hours, agonizing over a kid I was unable to reach. Being a teacher can be painful . . . at times it doesn't feel as if I'm reaching as many students as I succeed with." How can great teachers tolerate such angst?

Perhaps because the meaning of life is not so much in the objectives as in the process; in the journey rather than the destination. Before you decide to be one of the great teachers, you should mark the distinction between what is said about them and what they say about themselves. The anecdotal evidence suggests that instead of basking in the glory of their reputations as great teachers, they are more preoccupied with their failures and how they might do better.

YOU MAY BE CONSIDERED ARROGANT BY THE JEALOUS— LIVE WITH IT

None of the thirty-two great teachers focused on in this study were found to claim that they were great teachers. Their greatness was the accusation of others. Nonetheless, great teachers have ideas about how they approach educational issues, and that relative confidence can cause envy and resentment in others. If you decide to be one of the great teachers, you will not likely announce your intention aloud, but your work will create its own impression. You will, then, most likely be considered arrogant by the jealous—live with it.

ENEMIES OF EXCELLENCE ABOUND

Perhaps Noman has convinced you that should you undertake the odyssey of great teaching, the forces of good will rally to help you. Not. Rafe Esquith (2003) warns that the enemies of excellence abound. Esquith (2003:21, 34–35) describes this fact of life quite clearly, "The musician told the student, 'Well, there are no short cuts' . . . But the warning is here for all you young teachers who dare to be first rate—there will be many who will try to stop you. Outstanding teaching will require you not only to do everything in your power to reach your students, but to battle forces that are supposed to be on your side . . . it's not unusual for people more concerned with money, politics, and power to hinder the efforts of dedicated teachers. So be prepared for battle, unless you want to be like everyone else."

He continues with the seriousness of his warning, "You're on a roll. The kids are excited and can't wait for you to lead them on a journey to excellence. I have to give you some bad news. Even if you get to this point, the worst is yet to come (2003:109). . . . the forces of mediocrity aren't content with being mediocre; they'll do everything in their power to prevent even the humblest of teachers and children from accomplishing anything extraordinary" (110). "However, if you care about what you're doing, it's one of the toughest jobs around. If you care, and if your eyes are wide open, beware: your school is filled with bad guys" (184). Yet Esquith, as do other great teachers who can find a workable place, time, and assignment, prevails, and it is assuredly because the teaching and learning transcend such hard realities.

OUTSIDE OF CLASS YOU WILL HAVE MORE TROUBLE LIVING IN THE MOMENT AS YOU FIND YOURSELF PONDERING YOUR CLASS

No good deed goes unpunished. Goodness needs to be its own reward because great teaching receives virtually no external rewards, usually costs the teacher additional money out of his/her own pocket, draws criticism, jealousy, and resentment. With their eyes on the prize, on most days great teachers focus on the intrinsic rewards that come after the tears, heartache, and tiredness.

You may not want to be a great teacher. If you seem to work harder than most, the intrinsic satisfactions usually outweigh the costs, but as perhaps is true with other professions, you will probably find yourself preoccupied with your thoughts about your classes, often at the expense of your full attention to other aspects of your life, including too often to your most significant others. As Rafe Esquith (2007:199) observes about himself and how teaching can become somewhat obsessive: "If a good new song or a classic from the past finds its way to my ears, I can't simply listen and enjoy it. I'm always evaluating a song's potential for use with my students." Great teachers may well be warned to "get a life."

You may also create resentment among lesser lights that resent your apparent success, your independence, and your raising the bar for what they might otherwise feel obliged to work toward. You also have to stare failure in the face moment by moment; otherwise you will not make necessary adjustments, which is only less pleasant than failing to make those adjustments. You may also have to confront on a regular basis what you least like about yourself. Finally, you invited the load of frustration that comes with the likelihood of never quite feeling that you have accomplished all that you might. Even with you, great teacher that you might be, it remains true that no student truly had the teacher s/he deserved, not the least of which is because no one is perfect.

Were you born to be a great teacher? Yes. Since this is an art than can never be mastered, the key ingredients are will, and the will power to open yourself up to your students, accept what you find, and then take them further than they otherwise had realized was possible. Repeat: You are never prepared for the amount of failure in teaching, but its lessons are the lessons for great teachers.

Student teacher Judy Brown blurted out the truth of the matter to anyone who would listen in her student-teaching teacher education class: "You are never prepared for the amount of failure." Worth repeating: you are never prepared for the amount of failure in teaching. Yet the recognition of the failures is always the starting place for great teachers. Rafe Esquith observes in his *Teach Like Your Hair's on Fire* (2007: 224), "It's a thankless job . . . and it doesn't get easier. When you glance at your mental ledger, the red ink completely dominates the black. For every reason to believe, for every child you may help, there are dozens who make you want to give up." For a great teacher like Esquith, those feelings of wanting to give up are also the starting place for the renewal of the effort to try something else—not to give up teaching, but to give up what did not work.

That same sort of near obsessiveness was endemic to Sylvia Ashton-Warner's work that she described in her book, *Teacher* (1963). "I was still awake until about four in the morning over the June incident" (131). "I could never consider a day's work complete without an outburst somewhere" (147). "I'm tired these evenings" (165). Such struggles did not end with her move to an American school. "There are times when I can't teach, and this is one of them. There are troughs in effort as well as peaks and this is one of them" (1972:200). Nor did her fame, nor her persistence, prevent an institutional collapse. "School is closing" (1972:223). Eventually neither success nor failure is the primary consideration; the transcendence is in the engagement and the desire for true excellence. Approximations of greatness have to be good enough.

Chapter Six

What Might Keep You from Becoming a Great Teacher?

The following include ample reasons not to be a great teacher. Unless these factors are deeply considered, the discussion of great teachers as it pertains to you will be mere sophistry.

SYSTEMIC KNOWLEDGE

You will first need enough systemic knowledge to teach effectively. All teachers must be able to manage the day-to-day functions of the classroom. Not until prospective teachers have become competent at handling the basics of discipline and classroom management are they really able to consider the more noble reasons for teaching presumably covered in their teacher preparation program.

According to Jay Mathews's account in the book, *Escalante*, math teacher Ben Jimenez did not create great teaching at Garfield High School until he had sought out help from Jaime Escalante on handling the day-to-day demands of his lessons and his discipline. All great teachers had to learn to manage their classes.

THE MOST IMPORTANT KNOWLEDGE

The most important knowledge you need is of your students, and this cannot be gained until your class actually begins. In turn, this book can only give you ideas to think about up front for matching your capabilities with your students' interests and needs and in establishing propensities and places to look for trying to understand the particulars (and peculiarities) of your own students. This book argues that those students, your students, have the critical knowledge that you will need, and being ready to react to them is the truest key to being a great teacher.

> Substantial teacher development comes from using the lives of children as a rich source of study. Star teachers are constantly involved in learning more about their children, their families and communities, and what it means to grow up in particular settings. By using children's life experiences as a fundamental part of the classroom program, teachers continually learn more about children and community cultures. Teachers attribute almost all they know about child development to what they have learned about the lives of their students. Much teacher development comes from the process of sharing their own interests, experiences, and talents with their students. The children, in effect, reward and shape their teachers by accepting and affirming what they share. The teachers, in turn, see the need for children to share their own backgrounds. (Haberman, in Cochran-Smith, 2008:363–65)

Fortunately, getting to know one's students becomes the substance of great teaching and great personal growth.

KNOWLEDGE OF THE PEER GROUP

The great teacher has, or develops, a very savvy understanding of their students' peer group. Lesser teachers often take the infractions of youth personally, but the great teacher will recognize how classroom negotiations are very dependent upon working successfully with the peer group so that the students themselves adopt higher expectations for themselves.

Talcott Parsons's article (1968:78), "The School Class as a Social System" in *Harvard Educational Review*, Reprint Series #1, offers some relevant insights into the importance of the student peer group and its implications for the classroom teacher. Parsons says that "the importance of the peer group for socialization in our type of society should be clear. The motivational foundations of character are inevitably first laid down through identification with parents, who are generational superiors, and the generation difference is a type example of a hierarchical status difference. But an immense part of the individual's adult role performance will have to be in association with status-equals or near-equals." The parents and teachers, for example, can want or even expect that students become leaders, but leadership skills cannot be developed except though independent actions among peer equals.

Leslie Hart has found that students tend to learn more through talking than listening. Some lecture by the teacher may be necessary, but students will learn more about the subject by having the opportunity to speak about it and can learn the social skills associated with adult performance by having opportunities to work with other students in small groups in and outside of class.

Even with great teachers who do not incorporate as much group work, they respect and appreciate the sensitive transactions taking place among students and are cautious about advertently or inadvertently causing any damage to the relationships among students. Great teachers have such caution because "the youth culture is also a field for practicing the assumption of higher-order responsibilities, for conducting delicate human relations without immediate supervision and learning to accept the consequences" (Parsons, 1968:88).

By suitably challenging not only the individual student but also the peer group itself, the great teacher creates an environment in which students may very well find themselves in need of each other to meet unprecedented demands placed upon them. An interdependent response to a great teacher requires a growth in maturity that a dependence upon the teacher would not. For students to help each other capably in this new "field for practicing," the raised level of academic expectation requires them to interrelate more delicately.

Because the great teacher recognizes the necessary independence of the peer group, the great teacher does not confuse questioning authority with challenging authority, and in either instance makes every attempt not to take questioning or challenging personally. Students must necessarily learn their limitations by testing the limits. Parsons (1968:88) adds that "most adolescents do a certain amount of experimenting with the borderline of the unacceptable patterns; that they should do so is to be expected in view of the pressure toward independence from adults, and of the 'collusion' which can be expected in the reciprocal stimulation of age-peers."

Getting rid of a problem student rarely gets rid of an underlying class problem. One way or the other, classes choose at least one member to test a teacher's boundaries. If the student chosen to do the testing of the teacher were to be dropped from the class, the class has information about what caused that student to be dismissed, but if questions remain about the credibility or authority of that teacher, at least one more student will step forward to test that authority in yet another way. The "collusion" is not really negative, but informative, until the teacher has demonstrated a clear ability to handle everything that comes up.

The great teacher recognizes how important it is to catch students in their miscreant, irresponsible behavior so that it does not escalate any further. The great teacher recognizes the difference between ordinary student behaviors, which need not be perfect, and behavior that tests the limits. When tested the teacher does not do the students a favor by ignoring it; such a laissez-faire response only raises the ante for the next test.

As Parsons (1968:77) observes, "On the one hand, the peer group may be regarded as a field for the exercise of independence from adult control; hence it is not surprising that it is often a focus of behavior which goes beyond independence from adults to the range of adult-disapproved behavior; when this happens, it is the seed bed from which the extremists go over into delinquency." For example, what in the world was that "good kid" doing drinking hard liquor on campus? When lesser offenses go unchecked, the student will likely push the limits further until s/he discovers what the real limits are. Unsanctioned irresponsible behavior is the seedbed for delinquency, even among the students the school might think of as "the good kids."

However, the focus on what might become delinquent behavior does not do justice to the positive possibilities of the peer group. Parsons (1968:77) then adds, "But another very important function is to provide the child with a source of non-adult approval and acceptance. Thus the adult parents are augmented by age-peers as a source of rewards for performance and of security in acceptance."

A great teacher helps the student peer group grow into an independent source of support that can inculcate educational aspirations in ways that neither the parents nor teacher can match. Jaime Escalante was superior at doing this. While Escalante deserves the credit for his great success with Advanced Placement Calculus at Garfield High School, he could not have possibly had that success if he had not worked with the students as an independent peer group to internalize the high standards necessary for such work commitments and achievement results.

A great teacher works on helping the peer group decide on its own terms that the academic work is meaningful, worth the extra time and effort, and that the students must work closely together to ensure their own success. A great teacher does not tend to appreciate a student working to please the teacher. A great teacher appreciates a cohort of students agreeing that they are capable of raising their level of achievement, and working hard to make it so. The great teacher does not burden students with busy work; the great teacher creates a situation in which the student peer group will enforce the normative expectations that quality work is presumed and that anything less is as upsetting to the peer group as to the teacher.

YOUR BIOGRAPHY

[Frustratingly my student-teachers] picked and chose what content they would respond to in the course I taught based upon often unarticulated assumptions or "implicit theories" about teaching, learning, and themselves as teacher. They embraced activities and content that confirmed their prejudices and ignored, or more accurately, suffered through and then discounted, that which was contrary to these prejudices. (Bullough, 1994:107–21)

Is it possible for you to suspend your own biography long enough to recognize and do something about the limitations that you have constantly, advertently and inadvertently, imposed upon yourself? As an adult, you have spent your years "individuating." Now the challenge is to open yourself, as nonjudgmentally as feasible, to the life experiences of your students. Again, most do not make this transition, and the research shows, for example, that such adult teachers tend to have lower academic expectations for students with different backgrounds than their own. Consider the following challenge of the importance of teachers opening themselves to the potential of all their students.

Current scholarship suggests that teachers need to be knowledgeable about the social lives of the children and the conditions of their lives outside of school. What teachers know about the lives of children outside of school affects their pedagogical practices . . . In light of the diversity that is inherent in all classrooms, having the means to construct knowledge about differences among learners may be more important and less problematic than having information in learners in prepackaged forms . . . Teachers need to be reflective practitioners . . . working with learners whose experiences may be very different from their own requires teachers to confront unexamined beliefs and assumptions they have about students in relation to particular institutional practices and procedures that may serve as barriers to the equitable treatment of students. As students also have beliefs and assumptions about themselves and their capabilities, teachers need to help students make these transparent. To help students challenge their prescriptions of self, teachers need to be sensitive to the students' experiences of schooling and the curriculum, including classroom interactions with teachers and peers. Teachers are also advocates. They need to respond to diversity in ways that protect the rights of learners to an equal educational opportunity within the context of institutional racism. (Mercado in Richardson, 2001:690–91)

Ordinarily the challenge for introspection posed by the quotation goes unmet. White teachers are more likely than teachers of color to hold lower expectations for black and Latino students. White teachers often have more difficulty forming constructive relationships with students of color and are unable to build bridges between students and curriculum; they then interpret students' lack of engagement as disinterest in learning, or their academic problems as an inability to learn. Preservice students commonly bring into teacher education attitudes and experiences that eventually lead to the unfortunate patterns described above.

You will have spent your first twenty-one years of life getting clear on who you are and what your preferences will be. Now, as a teacher, you will be best served by opening yourself to appreciating the very different preferences of each and every one of your students. Fortunately enough, life will be richer this way.

YOUR STRENGTHS ARE MOST LIKELY YOUR WEAKNESSES

This statement applies both personally and professionally. For example, one's strength of character can be intimidating to some students; love for the subject matter may attract only the students who have that subject's peculiar way of doing things. Clayton Christensen explains how "subject matters" exclude most students:

> What happens then in the typical classroom is a kind of "reverse magnetic attraction." Every magnet, you may remember, has a positive and negative pole. Like poles repel each other, and opposite poles attract. In the typical classroom, those "like poles"—similar types of intelligence—attract, rather than repel, each other. This reverse magnetic attraction creates a vicious cycle. The teachers in classrooms are products of the monolithic batch-processing system that characterizes public education today. In that system, students who naturally enjoy the teaching approach they encounter in a given class are more likely to excel. For example, the subject material in a high school language arts class relates in obvious ways to linguistic intelligence. Students with that intelligence type naturally comprise most of the ones who excel in language arts. They're the ones who choose to major in that subject in college and then choose teaching careers in that field. Specific subject matter tends to be linked to specific intelligences through the way textbooks are written—by experts strong in that specific intelligence type. As a result, what has emerged in every domain is "intellectual cliques," composed of curriculum developers, teachers, and the best students in that subject area. Their brains are all wired consistently with each other. Just as members of a social clique often are unaware of the degree to which they easily understand and communicate with each other to the exclusion of those outside the group, members of these intellectual cliques are often unaware of the extent to which their shared patterns of thinking exclude those with strengths in other kinds of inteiiigences. Students not endowed with strong linguistic intelligence are therefore predictably frustrated in an English class. Teachers are similarly trapped by their own strengths. In any given classroom there are students who do not have strong linguistic intelligence and are therefore effectively excluded from excelling in this subject. And the pattern repeats itself from generation to generation. The same

happens in each of the academic disciplines. For example, teachers who teach math tend to have high logical-mathematical intelligence, and therefore the students who excel in their classes also tend to have this type of intelligence. Many other students are excluded. (2008:36–37)

A great math teacher will find a way for all students to learn without compromising the expectations of excellence.

NOMAN AND THE WAY IT SPOZED TO BE

Why do teachers continue to do things that do not work? Jim Herndon explains that "Noman" (literally No Man, but a nod at how teachers have been socialized in sometimes irrational ways) told us to do it the "way it spozed to be," the conventional way, even if reason tells the teacher it is not working. It is almost baffling how powerful Noman is and how difficult it is to ignore him. But great teachers do.

RECOGNIZING YOUR OWN VISION

Each time that teachers hold conferences with students, grade papers, ask students to explain their answers, or use results from a quiz to reorganize instruction, they are either following in the rut of existing practices and beliefs or participating in transforming the culture of the classroom. (Shepard in Richardson, 2001:1097)

As Pogo said, "We have met the enemy and they is us." What will it take to avoid the rut to be a great teacher? As Rafe Esquith has documented so effectively, any attempt at greatness will be met with great adversity. Emerson's essay on *Self-Reliance* affirms the necessity of finding one's own vision and can be a therapeutic read for the frustrated great teacher.

THE DEFAULT POSITION

"The default position" summarizes the greatest threat to all effective teaching. In the absence of any alternative approach a teacher tends to defer to their personally preferred modus operandi. Which will, of course, have very limited results with a diverse group of students.

Deferring to one's default position invariably delimits students to their detriment. The good news about having had an academic major in college to teach to one's own students is that the teacher is knowledgeable about that subject. However, the tendency, then, is to teach that subject only in the manner that students who share similar interests and traditional approaches to the subject will prefer. Being an enthusiastic teacher of that subject helps a bit, but such enthusiasm can be off-putting to those students of different interests and who prefer different approaches.

The probability is that not one student that a teacher has in a given academic year will go on to college and major in that subject. Thus a more educational approach to the teaching subject and student would emphasize finding answers to the question: What does everyone need, and perhaps even want, to know about this subject?

The default position is relevant to each and every teacher preference, decision, and practice. Not only the subject matter. Whatever the teacher's default position, some students do better in a discipline system that emphasizes rules and penalties, while others do better with norms and sanctions. Some students prefer to listen; others to read to learn new subject matter. Some students like to look the teacher in the eye; others do not. Some students tolerate ambiguity well; others do not. Some students prefer the responsibility of their own "internal locus of control," whereas others respond to the impingement of an "external locus of control." Some students see a scolding as caring, while others see it as a lack of caring. Some students like a pat on the back, but not every student.

Without dedication and close introspection, teachers will tend to rely upon the default position of their own personal preferences, regardless of what might actually better suit the teachers' particular class and students. Even if the single teacher's default position was somehow the best possible position, unless accommodation is made for the range of students, each student will have stunted educational opportunity.

Eventually a teacher cannot be all things to all students, but the teacher does need to closely inspect her/his default position and devise a strategy for best accommodating students with different preferred ways of doing things.

Chapter Seven

Conclusion about Being One of the Great Teachers

The specifics of what worked for other great teachers will not work for you. Units on dinosaurs, the Bible, Shakespeare, key vocabulary, and more that sound great in a great teacher's book will not work for you. Only what you can love, what you believe in, what you can make work . . . the question is always, "What can I make work with my students?"

The long-term best interests of your students must prevail. The crucible lies in the gap between what the student wants to hear and needs to hear. A great teacher can always be on the side of the student, while always telling them the truth.

THE CHALLENGE

All teaching is a great challenge, but great teaching requires teachers to go so far beyond their comfort levels. Failure and frustration are heightened, but the stretching and growth offer incomparable rewards.

A COMPARATIVE ASSESSMENT OF TWO OF THIS WORK'S GREAT TEACHERS BASED ON THE GREAT TEACHING INDICES

Great teachers cross grade and school levels and subject matters; they do not use the same approaches to curriculum or pedagogy. But they share common characteristics in terms of the response of students, their qualities as teachers, and their interaction with students. On the basis of Houston Peterson's work, how do teachers John M. Daly and Elliot Eisner fare in a competition on these characteristics of great teachers? For this "contest" the characteristics are given in the order originally identified by Houston Peterson.

The Sixteen Characteristics by Which to Evaluate

1. *Awakened aroused*, startled the student *into thought*.
2. Generated *contagious enthusiasm* among the students, creating an environment of a larger knowledge and a firmer purpose.
3. Had *no fear of feeling* and did *not attempt to achieve that specious academic objectivity that can freeze a class*.
4. Had *thorough knowledge of the subject* whether that *means* by *scholarship or* by personal *research*; an *original and penetrating intelligence; played easily with facts and ideas*.
5. *Carried students beyond* the subject's *boundaries*; created an atmosphere of learning for learning's sake; had a formative influence on students' educational identities.
6. Had a *rich fund* of example, metaphor, story to *make the complex more simple* and to *make learning meaningful*.
7. Limited the *insulation* between the teacher and student in some meaningful way.
8. *Always had one eye on the classroom, the other forever on the community*; gave students a *sense of* what was *going on "outside."*
9. Was the *"best" teacher*, not necessarily *the most "finished" teacher*, often working *through ideas struggling for expression*, rather than simply presenting preformulated ones; *exhibited an original and penetrating intelligence at work, playing freely with facts and ideas*.
10. Made students think independently; *stimulated independence of investigation by questions and suggestions*; *gave high importance to establishing habits of self-reliance*; encouraged an *exchange of ideas*; made students *ask and answer questions*; sowed the seeds of students' *intellectual* and imaginative life; *initiated inquiry*; developed *intellectual curiosity*.
11. Intellectually challenging and rigorous (*not to work much, but well*); broke down resistance to new *ideas*; created an atmosphere that issues were serious and personal; daunting only such that students rose to the challenge; contended, struggled, encountered students (and any smugness of self-satisfactions), challenging and inspiring them to their best work; not readily satisfied, raised the bar; set higher (but with great effort) reachable standards.
12. Had, cultivated, and understood the worth of creating a (unique) teaching *"personality"*; created a *"presence."*

13. Maintained a certain relationship with students, *not affection*, but probably a respect that had a *personal element*.
14. Sought to impact each and every student in the class.
15. Had a sense of *complete freedom from academic provincialism*; had a mind characterized as having been *washed clean of scholastic dust*; had something *of a quite jolly air of conscious insubordination*, the mind impatiently dismissing the *solemn snobbery of all that is academically canonized and sacrosanct.*
16. Had a certain kind of *knowledge of individual students*; knew which buttons to press to inculcate student growth.

Bill James has made a name for himself as a baseball writer by trying to find numerical methods for perspective on his subjective opinions. Was Mickey Mantle or Willie Mays the greatest centerfielder of that era? Reducing all the statistics to one that predicts "game wins," James found that Mantle had the greatest peak, but Mays the greater career.

The historical records of teachers yield no such data to make such determination, but on the basis of known evidence John M. Daly won the assessment competition over Elliot Eisner by a single point. While Peterson's set of the characteristics of great teachers has been found to be interesting and a way of assessing how great teachers do things differently, a one-point distinction is hardly decisive. But using the characteristics better to appreciate these two great teachers was, nonetheless, instructive.

How did Daly, the high school Honor's History teacher, happen to best the renowned university professor Elliot Eisner? The best answer, of course, is that he did not. As has been said about comparing the *Mona Lisa* to any other classic work of art—"there's no competition among the classics."

Nonetheless, allowing ten points for each of the sixteen characteristics, Eisner scored a one-point advantage on #9. Eisner was wondrous as he struggled to bring ideas to life in the classroom. However, Daly earned the slight edge on #13 and #15. It may be that he benefited in this regard from having been the high school teacher. He clearly knew how to push student buttons, and perhaps this was possible because he spent so many more classroom hours with a student than a university professor would. Because of the greater amount of contact, he also had much more opportunity to involve himself with each and every student. So there you have it—Daly by a nose.

The comparison and contrast between Daly and Eisner affirmed that Peterson's list of the characteristics can be used meaningfully and relevantly across subject and school levels in identifying what distinguishes great teachers. However, the results of the Eisner and Daly "competition" also indicate that apparent differences among great teachers may be related to factors such as the year in school of the students that they teach.

Meanwhile, such an informal assessment based on these sixteen characteristics tends to demonstrate the utility of helping one think more insightfully about great teachers. This seems to be true for thinking about the special qualities of the great teachers you have hopefully had. Quite possibly such an assessment could become part of the teacher evaluation process, establishing evidence and support for those teachers who dare to rise to the challenge to be great. The identification of these characteristics improves the possibilities of encouraging each generation of teachers who face the same resistance all such teachers have faced since Socrates. Great teachers face the accusations of corrupting the minds of the youth, when in fact their real threat is merely disturbing the status quo.

WHAT SORT OF THINGS DO STUDENTS WRITE ABOUT GREAT TEACHERS?

How Great Teachers Set High Standards

"The intellectualism of the course is really unmatched by others."

"(The teacher) is challenging . . . forces (the) students to think critically."

"(The teacher) is hard on students in order to stimulate them."

"You are pushed in this class to back up your thoughts with evidence."

"(The teacher) will correct students without making them humiliated or making it personal."

"This is my most demanding course."

"I will most likely never have an A in this class, but I am always proud of my effort to learn."

"(The teacher) challenges me to think in new ways and push(es) my personal limits."

"Most intellectually demanding course that I have ever taken."

"(The teacher) is intense—makes the students actually read."

"Holds students accountable for being prepared."

"Challenges students to think more critically."

"Challenges students to do their best and maintains high expectations from everyone."

"Holds students to the highest possible standards of excellence."

"Makes me WANT to actually do my homework."

"Keeps you on your toes and forces you to read the books."

"Good at making you think critically."

"Has high expectations for students and genuinely wants all to do well."

Develop a Great Teacher Persona

"Things liked best about the (teacher): honesty and humor."

"Unconventional but highly effective."

"Unique teaching style."

"Things you like best about this (teacher): no-nonsense sensibility, dry sense of humor, challenging environment."

"(The teacher) is a paradox. Intimidating, but personable. Threatening, yet encouraging."

"Most engaged (teacher that) I have ever had."

"Passionate, fun, knowledgeable, humorous."

"Engaging and entertaining . . . making our retention levels very high."

"Upfront and honest . . . says what (s/he) thinks."

"(The teacher) is not afraid to do unique things."

"I love how different (the course) is."

"Incisive questioning."

"Loves what (s/he) is doing."

"Intuitive."

Uses the Curriculum and Hidden Curriculum

"(The teacher) forces . . . students (to be) responsible thinkers."

"Aristotle says 'Excellence is not an act; it is a habit.' So maybe it's not the class that is excellent, but what we will do with what we've learned from it."

"The discussion creates a need for responsibility to one's peers."

"Helps us develop into independent thinkers."

"Holds us accountable."

"Regards the subject with love and respect, and imparts that love and respect of great thought to students."

"This class helps students to develop their own worldview and moral standard."

Establish Relationships with Students

"Despite incredible knowledge (and) insight . . . he pushes students into their own understanding."

"(The teacher) cares about the students as people while still treating them with the respect of scholars."

"(The teacher) cares if the students develop traits needed to be good students, as well as good people."

"Able to connect with students."

"(The teacher) truly cares about (the) students and is willing to take time after class to guide and help us."

"Focuses on really having each of us really learn the material for ourselves."

"Respectful and sincere when talking to students."

"That demand for excellence is not extracted at the expense of egregious time-allocation or my grade. This is phenomenal."

"(The teacher) demands the highest possible standard of analysis while demonstrating (a) deep personal investment in each student."

"Engaged with the students on a personal level."

"I look forward to coming to class."

Use the Classroom as a Lab

"(The teacher) give(s) the class the freedom to follow the area of inquiry or creativity that they want."

"(The teacher) lets us discover the material for ourselves and reach conclusions based off of our understanding of course texts, but is there to correct us and bring up new aspects of the works that we might not have considered."

"(The teacher) mixes things up . . . approaches every class in a different way."

"Knows how to make complicated (ideas) easy and understandable."

"Knows how to tailor the class material so that people of different learning styles can benefit equally."

"(The teacher) knows how to explain difficult ideas and explain them in a way that everyone can understand."

"The course is . . . structured to allow students multiple avenues in which to demonstrate their aptitude."

"(The teacher) is always looking for more and better ways to teach."

"(The teacher) is devoted to doing everything (s/he) can to help each of (his/her) students learn in whatever way works for them."

"(The teacher) has a way of tailoring the class to each of (his/her) students."

Create a Sense of Community

"Even in the group setting (the teacher) is able to reach out to and teach individual students and the group comes together as a result."

"The class usually comes together to create understandings of ideas that often reach beyond individual ability, such a synergy often exists."

"I love finding new ways of understanding myself and the world around me."

"Things you liked best about the course: The people."

"(The teacher) kept in contact with (former students) after they (had taken the) class."

"I gained real knowledge . . . that will be with me my whole life."
"Makes us step outside our worldview and see how it appears to the rest
of the world."
"Taught me to think for myself while equipping me with tools that I
would need for the real world."
"Enhanced knowledge of the real world."

Earn Their Influence

"Helped me develop my sense of moral integrity and personal values."
"The best course I have taken . . . and the most relevant to life."
"This is THE class."

A MESSAGE TO ALL TEACHERS

Great teachers are necessarily a small minority because greatness is a com-
parative term and because having too many great teachers would probably
overload students. This need not be resented by other teachers. First, an
obvious reason for great teachers' distinction is not their fault. Humans tend
to make invidious comparisons that are not fair. A terrible major league
baseball player may have been the best from his home state the year of his
graduation from school. *Poor* and *great* tend to be relative terms compared to
the whole of any group. If a number of students think a teacher is somehow
better than the other teachers, arguing with such opinions seems beside any
point.

Second, Jay Mathews asked the question whether great teachers are born
or made. A third alternative exists. Perhaps great teachers were drafted. If
great teachers are thought to inspire great students, quite probably the corol-
lary is also true, that great students can inspire and even create great teachers.

Reportedly many of Jaime Escalante's students at Garfield High School
resented their stereotypical depictions in the Hollywood film, *Stand and
Deliver*. The actual students that took calculus from Escalante were not just
any students. They were promising students at a large comprehensive city
high school. If they had not yet realized great achievement, they were students of great aptitude and open to legitimate opportunity and to being moti-
vated to significant success. Their contributions to the growth of Escalante
and Jimenez as great teachers should not be overlooked or underappreciated.

Third, great teachers make everyone's job a little easier, not harder. Sure,
their example may create momentary guilt on the part of those working less
hard, or those not getting the credit they also deserve. But success tends to

breed success, and the presence of a high-achieving student group on campus raises the general standards of student responsibility, and the good press of success helps the reputation of the entire school.

Perhaps the human tendency is to complain, but if you have read this book and found its claims to be basically true, you can appreciate the high costs in time, energy, and commitment of the great teacher and be thankful for such a colleague for their efforts, and even that you do not have to be such a teacher to continue to be exceedingly important to your students and school.

A LETTER TO A YOUNG, GREAT TEACHER

You are smart, you care about your students, you do your best work when you are least worried about what you think you are "spozed" to be doing. You have spent thirty years preparing yourself. Trust your background, your experience, yourself, and your relationship with your students. Don't over-prepare; teach authentically, organically, in the moment. In terms of the canons of rhetoric, trust your memory to bring to mind what will seem fresh examples rather than rehearsed examples in your classroom discussions.

Research suggests that what the student does is more important to student learning than the teacher's performance, so don't obsess about yourself—pay even closer attention to your class. With rare exceptions you know more about your subject than your students will ever want to know, so focus on the most important stuff; teach less, better.

Certainly the preponderance of your work will be with moving your curriculum forward, but without guilt allow classroom time for class maintenance. Are students missing a reading skill? Not working harmoniously? Is a student dominating discussion? Are the desks too close together? Have the students hit a lull in the semester? Minutes spent solving such problems sustain the curriculum. While this may not seem an efficient use of classroom time, it is effective.

You will find your own way to meet the challenge of greatness, but perhaps this book has something that will speak to you. Bring out that aspect of your teaching persona that is the gadfly. Be more confident in your own observations of your classes instead of what you have been told is expected by others. And turn some of that great amount of time you spend with individual students into some sort of program, club, or undertaking that will give them a greater sense of being "in it together" in an important learning community.

SOCRATES AND THE LEGACY OF GREAT TEACHERS

A legacy is a gift handed down from the past. Ideas have a life of their own. One way or another all great teachers are indebted to the legacy of Socrates. Houston Peterson assembled his book on great teachers in 1946, but the birthdates of the twenty-two teachers identified in his book ranged from 1773 to 1865. This book argues that the same characteristics that typified great teachers in his book remain representative and relevant for understanding the greatness of the thirty-two teachers from this study.

That such characteristics should stand the test of time for the two hundred years of the teachers of those two books should be no surprise. They are the same characteristics exemplified by Socrates. Socrates and the other thirty-one teachers of this book were consistent in their use of teaching strategies and practices.

Socrates created a teaching persona that has remained fresh for over 2,500 years. He managed that dynamic mix of provoking and lovable. In the *Apology* Socrates (1992:31–32) admits: "I am that gadfly which God has given the state, and all day long and in all places am always fastening upon you, arousing and persuading and reproaching you." The persona that he created left an impression: "I met Socrates, he told me, looking very spruce after his bath, with a nice pair of shoes on although, as you know, he generally goes about barefoot. So I asked him where he was going, cutting such a dash" (Socrates, 1985:215).

Most likely he was headed off to engage in a meeting of minds. He was prone to starting his conversations with what must have obviously been playful modesty. Responding to what others had said, "There's not much left for me to say after the wonderful speech we've just had from Agathon . . . what chance have I or anyone of knowing what to say, after listening to such a flood of eloquence as that? . . . I personally, was so mortified when I compared it with the best that I could ever hope to do, that for two pins I'd have tried to sneak away" (Socrates, 1985:235–36).

Certainly he was not one to sneak away, but would turn such banter into a skewer:

"Their persuasive words almost made me forget who I was . . . yet they hardly spoke a word of truth" (Socrates, 1992:19). He might goad them with ironic understatement: "I take it then that what we undertook was to flatter, rather than to praise, the god of love, and that's why you're all prepared to say the first thing about him that comes into your heads" (Socrates, 1985:236).

Having established his right to tell the truth, he engaged in his method of dialogue. He described his method as "to introduce a confusion and uncertainty." He clarifies this by adding, "I show him that he is not wise; and this occupation quite absorbs me" (1985:24).

Students would soon realize that they had been too self-confidently on the wrong track: "I begin to be afraid, my dear Socrates, that I didn't know what I was talking about" (1992:240).

The basic content for his teaching revolved around this issue:

"A man who is good for anything ought not to calculate the chance of living or dying; he ought only to consider whether in doing anything he is doing right or wrong" (1992:29).

One of the costs of great teaching is distraction. Socrates was the absent-minded teacher challenged to stay in the moment. "As we went along Socrates fell into a fit of abstraction . . . it's quite a habit of his, you know; off he goes and there he stands, no matter where it is" (1992:216–17).

The greatest cost, of course, was his life. For all his good work he was found to be the "doer of evil and corrupter of youth" (1985:25). He was consequently sentenced to death, which came to him through the taking of hemlock. Although one rightly reflects upon his death as a tragic consequence of great teaching, he had taught for years on his own terms. He must have suffered in the more usual ways as other great teachers suffer. He offered the encouragement, "Pleasure comes following after the pain" (1985:58).

Implicitly and explicitly he responded to the challenge of greatness to be a great teacher. He responded to the lifelong demands of teaching: "This occupation quite absorbs me" (1985:24). He wanted no other vocation or avocation: "While I have life and strength I shall never cease from the practice (of) teaching" (1992:30).

The Challenge of Greatness: The Legacy of Great Teachers finds, if self-consciously, great enjoyment in Socrates' literal last laugh before his death by hemlock: "He added, laughing, I am speaking like a book, but I believe that what I am saying is true" (1985:100).

Alcibiades in *The Symposium* offers the eulogy for Socrates that could provide the substance for the eulogy for the great teachers within this book's pantheon of great teachers:

When we listen to anyone else talking, however eloquent he is, we don't really care a damn what he says. But when we listen to Socrates, or to someone else repeating what he's said, we are simply bewitched. I'd swear on oath what an extraordinary effect his words have had on me—and still do, if it comes to that. What extraordinary powers he has got. I've been bitten in the heart, or the mind, or whatever you like to call it, by Socrates.

There's a lot to be said about Socrates, all very peculiar and all very much to his credit. No doubt there's just as much to be said about any of his little ways, but personally I think the most amazing thing about him is the fact that he is absolutely unique; there's no one like him, and I don't believe there ever was. (1992:condensed from 259–67)

Socrates personified and defined the great teacher, but other great teachers like those identified in this book have continued the legacy. The eulogy for Socrates could be said about each teacher in this pantheon of great teachers.

FINAL WORDS

Why pay the price of being a great teacher? At times the art of teaching becomes a transcendent experience that elevates the soul. When does a great teacher's craft become art? Elliot Eisner says that this happens when the craft transcends its simple, practical functions, when it addresses the universals, when it is treasurable beyond its time and place, when it addresses the human condition, and when it is superlatively well done. Moments in the classroom take on this dimension. Eisner (1979:153–68) has identified four "senses" by which an activity can be considered an art.

Teaching is an art in the sense that it can be performed with such skill and grace that, for the student as well as the teacher, the experience can justifiably be characterized as aesthetic. What occurs is a "performance" that provides an intrinsic form of satisfaction. When the great teacher and students are caught up in the teaching-learning experience, the class may be described as having been a masterpiece.

Teaching is an art in the sense that the teacher makes judgments based on qualities that unfold during the course of action. Qualitative forms of intelligence are used to select, control, and organize the coverage of a class. The great teacher reads the emerging qualities of a particular class and responds with qualities appropriate to that particular class. In this process, qualitative judgment is exercised in the interests of achieving a qualitative end.

Teaching is an art in the sense that the activity is not dominated by prescriptions or routines but is influenced by qualities and contingencies that are unpredictable. The great teacher works in an innovative way to cope with these contingencies. Great teachers respond to the kind of day that they find, which can be influenced by the weather, a campus disturbance, the promise of a vacation coming up, or a student who has had a particularly good or bad day.

Teaching is an art in the sense that the ends are often created in process. Craft has been defined as the process through which skills are used to arrive at preconceived ends. Art has been defined as the process in which skills are used to discover ends through action. For the great teacher each class has the prospect of becoming something new, whether chronic, tragic, humorous, touching, parabolic, allegorical, or mundane. While not confined, or even particularly concerned about such matters as behavioral objectives and standardized testing, great teachers' students do well in such matters because the larger matters are so well attended.

At the artistic heights of such great teaching-learning the activity becomes characterized by what Mihaly Csikszentmihalyi (2008) describes as *flow*. Flow accounts for the manner in which a class can get caught up in the moment and transcend time and space, when the class becomes so involved that it has no sense of the day, hour, minute, or of even being confined to a classroom. Csikszentmihalyi's summative observation is that flow characterizes not only the great teacher as artist but also the teaching, and quite often the very experience of the students themselves. Csikszentmihalyi has limited his description of flow to the artist. The suggestion here is that the idea of flow applies equally well to the teaching, and quite often to the experience of the students.

Csikszentmihalyi discusses the artist when he says, "Integration refers to the extent to which the different parts communicate and enhance one another's goals. A system that is more differentiated and integrated than another is said to be more complex." That description certainly applies to the complexity of great teachers, and equally as well to their results that, finally, stand alone.

Csikszentmihalyi is aware that this characteristic of flow can be experienced by the "audience." He says, "Quite often people mention experiencing self-transcendence in flow, as when a musician playing a particularly beautiful melody feels at one with the order of the cosmos." While such experiences cannot be planned per se, they happen often enough to keep the great teacher continuing to seek out this particular experience of the world.

Great teachers share the aesthetic joys with other artists, while also knowing that with the ongoing relationship they develop with their students, that they have the prospects of simultaneously contributing to a legacy of student learning and growth. At least for the great teachers, this type of reward makes the failures, the adversity, the frustration, fraught with meaning instead of despair. Great teaching provides substantial sustenance.

Final four words: **Be good, teach great.**

References

Anyon, Jean. (1980). Social Class and the Hidden Curriculum of Work. *Journal of Education* 162(1): 67–92.

Apple, Michael, and Nancy R. King. (1977). What Do Schools Teach? In R. H. Weller (Ed.), *Humanistic Education: Vision and Realities* (pp. 27–47). Berkeley, CA: McCutchan.

Aristotle. (2002). In Joe Sachs (Trans.), *Nicomachean Ethics*. Newburyport, MA: Focus Publishing.

Ashton-Warner, Sylvia. (1963). *Teacher*. New York: Simon and Schuster.

Ashton-Warner, Sylvia. (1972). *Spearpoint: "Teacher" in America*. New York: Knopf.

Bain, Ken. (2004). What Makes Great Teachers Great? *Chronicle of Higher Education*, April 9, 2004. http://chronicle.com/article/What-Makes-Great-Teachers/31277.

Berlak, Ann, and Harold Berlak. (1981). *Dilemmas of Schooling: Teaching and Social Change*. New York: Methuen.

Braithwaite, E. R. (1959). *To Sir, with Love*. New York: Pyramid Books.

Buber, Martin. (1958). In Gregor Smith (Trans.), *I and Thou*. New York: 1958.

Bullough, Robert V. (1994). Personal History and Teaching Metaphors: A Self Study of Teaching as Conversation. *Teacher Education Quarterly* (Winter).

Burke, Edmund. (1988). In Edgar Knoebel (Ed.), *Classics of Western Thought*. New York: Harcourt, Brace, Jovanovich.

Buskist, William, Dale Smith, and Jared Keeley. (2006). The Teacher Behaviors Checklist: Factor Analysis of Its Utility for Evaluating Teaching. *Teaching of Psychology* 33(2).

Christensen, Clayton. (2008). *Disrupting Class: How Disruptive Innovation Will Change the Way the World Learns*. New York: McGraw Hill.

Coleman, Rhoda, and Claude Goldenberg. (2010). What Does Research Say about Effective Practices for English Learners? *Record* 46(1) (Summer).

Cronbach, Lee J., and Patrick Suppes. (1969). *Research for Tomorrow's Schools: Disciplined Inquiry for Education*. London: The Macmillan Company.

Csikszentmihalyi, Mihaly. (2008). *Flow: The Psychology of Optimal Experience*. New York: Harper.

Eisner, Elliot W. (1979). *The Educational Imagination: On the Design and Evaluation of School Programs*. New York: Macmillan.

Eisner, Elliot W. (1991). *The Enlightened Eye: Qualitative Inquiry and the Enhancement of Educational Practice*. New York: Macmillan.

Epstein, Joseph. (1981). *Masters: Portraits of Great Teachers*. New York: Basic Books.

Esquith, Rafe. (2003). *There Are No Short Cuts*. New York: Pantheon.

Esquith, Rafe. (2007). *Teach Like Your Hair's on Fire*. New York: Viking Press.

Freire, Paulo. (1970). *Pedagogy of the Oppressed*. New York: Continuum.

Fries, Maureen. (1992). Female Heroes, Heroines and Counter-Heroes: Images of Women in Medieval Arthurian Tradition. In Sally Slocum (Ed.), *Popular Arthurian Traditions* (pp. 5–17). Kentucky: Bowling Green State University Popular Press.

Gage, N. L., and D. C. Berliner. (1998). *Educational Psychology* (2nd Edition). Chicago: Houghton Mifflin.

Gose, Michael. (1999). *Creating a Winning Game Plan*. Thousand Oaks: Corwin Press.

Gose, Michael. (2005). Finding the Bottom Line: Teaching for Excellence, August.

Gose, Michael. (2006). *Getting Reel: A Social Science Perspective on Film*. Youngstown: Cambria Press.

Gose, Michael. (2011). *Quality Questions*. Unpublished study.

Haberman, Martin, and Linda Post. (2008). Teachers for Multicultural Schools: The Power of Selection. In Marilyn Cochran-Smith (Ed.), *Handbook of Research on Teacher Education*. New York: Routledge.

Herndon, James. (1965). *The Way It Spozed to Be*. New York: Bantam Books.

Herndon, James. (1971). *How to Survive in Your Native Land*. Portsmouth, NH: Boynton/ Cook.

Hunter, Elizabeth. (1972). *Encounter in the Classroom: New Ways of Teaching*. New York: Holt, Rinehart and Winston.

Inchausti, Robert. (1993). *Spitwad Sutras: Classroom Teaching as Sublime Vocation*. Westport: Bergin & Garvey.

Jackson, Philip. (1968). *Life in Classrooms*. New York: Holt, Rinehart and Winston.

Kohl, Herbert. (1967). *36 Children*. New York: Signet.

Ladson-Billings, Gloria. (2009). *The Dreamkeepers: Successful Teachers of African American Children*. San Francisco: Jossey-Bass.

Liesveld, Rosanne, and Jo Ann Miller. (2005). *Teach with Your Strengths: How Great Teachers Inspire Their Students*. New York: Gallup Press.

Mathews, Jay. (1988). *Escalante: The Best Teacher in America*. New York: Henry Holt.

Mathews, Jay. (2009). *Work Hard. Be Nice. How Two Inspired Teachers Created the Most Promising Schools in America*. New York: Algonquin Books.

McLellan, Jeffrey, and Mary Jo V. Pugh. (1999). *The Role of Peer Groups in Adolescent Social Identity: Exploring the Importance of Stability and Change*. San Francisco: Jossey Bass.

Mercado, Carmen. (2001). The Learner: "Race," "Ethnicity," and Linguistic Difference. In Virginia Richardson (Ed.), *Handbook of Research on Teaching* (4th Edition). Washington, DC: AERA.

Morgan, Norah, and Juliana Saxton. (2004). Taxonomy of Personal Engagement. In Jackie Walsh (Ed.), *Quality Questioning: Research-Based Practice to Engage Every Learner* (pp. 124–25). Thousand Oaks: Corwin Press.

O'Hair, Mary John, and Eero Ropo. (1994). Unspoken Messages: Understanding Diversity in Education Requires Emphasis on Nonverbal Communication. *Teacher Education Quarterly* 21(3) (Summer).

Oser, Fritz. (2001). AERA Choreographies of Teaching. In Virginia Richardson (Ed.), *Handbook of Research on Teaching*. Washington DC: AERA.

Parsons, Talcott. (1968). The School Class as a Social System. *Harvard Educational Review*, Reprint Series #1, pp. 69–90.

Pascarelli, Ernest. (2005). *How College Affects Students*. San Francisco: Jossey-Bass.

Peterson, Houston. (1946). *Great Teachers*. New Brunswick: Rutgers University Press.

Practical Theory.org. (2004). What Makes a Great Teacher? Friday, August 22, 2003. http://practicaltheory.org/serendipity/index.php?archives/8-What-makes+a-great-teacher.htm.

Richardson, Virginia (Ed.). (2001). *Handbook of Research on Teaching*. Washington DC: AERA.

Sawyer. (2004). March. http://www.aera.net/uploadedfiles/journals_and_publications/journals/educational_researcher/volume_33_no_2/2026-03_sawyer.pdf.

Shaftel, Fannie. (1967). *Role-Playing for Social Values: Decision-Making in the Social Studies*. Englewood Cliffs: Prentice-Hall.

Shepard, Lorrie. (2001). The Role of Classroom Assessment in Teaching and Learning. In Virginia Richardson (Ed.), *Handbook of Research on Teaching* (4th Edition). Washington, DC: AERA.

Slavin, Robert. (2009). *Educational Psychology*. Columbus: Pearson.

Socrates. (1985). *The Symposium: Great Books Reading and Discussion Program*. Chicago: Great Books Foundation.

Socrates. (1992). *Plato: The Trial and Death of Socrates, Four Dialogues*. New York: Dover Publications.

Szymborska, Wislawa. (1996). Nobel Lecture, December 7, 1996. http://www.nobelprize.org/nobel_prizes/literature/laureates/1996/szymborska-lecture.html?print=1.

Talmadge, Harriet. Social Class

Tolstoy, Leo. (1967). *On Education*. Chicago: University of Chicago Press.

Tyack, David. (1974). *The One Best System: A History of American Urban Education*. Cambridge: Harvard University Press.

Tyler, Ralph. (1950). *Basic Principles of Curriculum and Instruction*. Chicago: University of Chicago Press.

Wallis, Claudia. (2008). How to Make Great Teachers. *Time*, Wednesday, February 13. http://www.time.com/time/magazine/article/0,9171,1713473,00.html.

Whitaker, Todd. (2004). *What Great Teachers Do Differently: 14 Things That Matter Most*. New York: Eye on Education.

Wise, Tim. (2011). *White Like Me: Reflections on Race from a Privileged Son*. New York: Soft Skull Press.

Appendix

CAVEATS

1. The context of deep appreciation for great teachers.

I discuss great teachers in the context of deep appreciation for all teachers. My previous book, *What It Means to Be a Teacher*, celebrates the commonalities among teachers. On the basis of much good teaching a relative small percentage of my own teachers made a critical difference to my long-term educational aspirations. Having had perhaps 150 teachers or more from kindergarten through graduate school, the twelve teachers that I had that I find meet Peterson's definition of greatness represent a healthy 8 percent of my own classroom experience. If everyone was so lucky and great teachers happened to be evenly distributed, students could certainly expect to encounter at least one great teacher by the time of high school graduation.

Anecdotally it would seem that it takes only one great teacher to make a significant difference for an individual student. While the emphasis of this study is upon great teachers, their work is dependent upon the good work of other teachers and a measure of institutional stability so that their work can be undertaken and sustained. A former administrator myself, I am probably somewhat overly critical of administrators who fail to support great teachers but very respectful of the preponderance of teaching professionals.

In my previous book cited above I recount the tale of the teacher whom most thought to be the worst on a teaching staff, who nonetheless had her own cadre of appreciative students with whom she had worthy success. The acclaim that comes to great teachers does not have to diminish the respect for the countless good and excellent teachers, who quite reasonably do not choose to make the sacrifices made by the great teachers.

2. Not everyone needs to be a great teacher.

A group of honors students were once coaxed into taking four great teachers all at the same time. Overload. One great teacher at a time seems to be preferable, but meanwhile a student needs to progress academically, studying other subjects with good teachers who may be making fewer demands upon a student's larger vision of a purposeful education.

At Garfield High School most of Jaime Escalante's students did not have sufficient time to undertake other Advanced Placement classes, yet they still needed to earn the other credits for high school graduation and college admission. At Mission Bay High School, Tom Goodwin elected to emphasize his work with his math teacher, Granny Smith, rather than endure the challenges of John M. Daly. Great teachers expect, even demand, students to engage in reflective thought, and too many great undertakings at once may short-circuit each other.

3. Choosing to read this book is an indication that you have the resolve, commitment, openness, and will power to become a great teacher.

This book finds and argues that obvious charisma is common among great teachers, but it is not a prerequisite. Two of the teachers in this study, Frank Corcoran and Ben Jimenez, were both seen as unassuming and even shy. Anyone willing to consider being a teacher has something special; what becomes essential is getting in touch with what is special, committing to doing what is actually best for each student's long-term best interests, maintaining this commitment against predictable adversity, and finding what is special within each student. What makes each great teacher special is unique, but each teacher candidate has something, which if developed, can be comparably special. What all great teachers share is courage and commitment.

4. You undoubtedly know the world needs great teachers, either because you had one or because you did not.

Hopefully you had a great teacher, someone to appreciate even more deeply because of your reflection on how they met the criteria established by Houston Peterson. If you were not so fortunate, you most likely can imagine what such a teacher must be like and know that far beyond how you did on standardized testing is how important a great teacher might be to a richer education and its influence on a deeper appreciation of life.

5. Can a great prophet come from Bethlehem?

Apparently so. The greatest teacher that I know of personally was not from an Ivy League school but did his work at a community college and a state school. One of his distinct advantages was his having been the student of one of the other great teachers in this book's study. Great teachers come from unlikely places, or perhaps it might be more aptly put that greatness only comes from unlikely places.

Who would have expected the founders of the inner-city Knowledge Is Power Program (KIPP) schools to come from privileged Ivy League backgrounds? The legendary American Calculus teacher to hail from Bolivia? For Sylvia Ashton-Warner to do her best work in New Zealand? Thus where you are from is exactly where you needed to come from to realize your transcendent greatness.

Personal experience emphasizes this point. I had been the Director of Secondary Education at Pepperdine University, and then became the Chair of the Social Science/Teacher Education Division. I had the greatest respect for my colleagues in Teacher Education and was not an administrator likely to intervene on behalf of a teaching candidate who was being dropped from the Teacher Education program. She was having a lot of failure, but what impressed me was her willingness to learn from it. It was the one time in my career that I intervened to the extent that I asked the co-coordinator to reconsider the decision to drop this student, knowing that I lacked sufficient evidence to make such a request. I worried and fretted that I was making a huge mistake.

Two years later that same teacher candidate had become a credentialed teacher and had become the teacher of the year in her district. I do not desire the credit for any special wisdom in this case, for I truly wondered whether I was right. The case did confirm what I had only been dimly aware of, that one of the very best indicators of a great teacher is that person who looks failure directly in the face and adjusts, adjusts, adjusts. This same teacher, from a very protected background, happened to go on to work closely with gangs and to determine how gangs affect school and classroom life. This is the exemplar of great teachers: the commitment and the willingness to learn from failure distinguish great teachers, especially early in their careers.

BIASES OF THE STUDY

Professors Elliot Eisner and Elizabeth Cohen recommend that authors be as transparent as possible with a study's biases, and that is taken as good advice.

> Craft knowledge is rooted in its own epistemology—an epistemology of practice and action—and that the epistemology of practice is largely incommensurable with the theory-oriented ways of knowing that are so prized in universities and similar sorts of settings. (Schon in Richardson, 2001:180)

At the top of his list of the characteristics of great teachers, Houston Peterson lists that a great teacher must have "had no fear of feeling and did not attempt that specious academic objectivity which can freeze a class." While seeking to be truthful, this book does not purport to be objective. The following considerations ought to be taken into account while reading this book:

- Elliot Eisner argues that scientists tend to be preoccupied with finding truth, artists with finding meaning.
- By Eisner's explication of "empirical," this book is empirical in that it is based in experience.
- Lee J. Cronbach considers research to include any disciplined inquiry of an academic concern.
- Using a very Aristotelian approach, this book makes a distinction between great teachers and great teaching.

I mention these considerations to establish clearly the biases of which I am most aware that affect the nature of this study. While I have reason to believe that all of the teachers included in this book might well be considered great teachers, I have no necessity to argue 1) that they always lived up to those characteristics (or sought to do so) delineated in this book, 2) that they did not have other traits that were important to their own teaching that are over-looked here, nor 3) do I have knowledge on whether they practiced great teaching over the entire length of their respective careers.

Arturo Pacheco's career led him to spend most of it in educational administration. Young great teachers John Holt, Jonathan Kozol, and Herb Kohl left the profession to become professional writers. Was Jaime Escalante as great a teacher after he moved from Garfield High School to Sacramento? Jim Herndon never described his teaching in ways that would stand out on Houston Peterson's list of characteristics, but Herndon's descriptions of his own classroom teaching gives ample evidence of his attention to his persona, his determination to learn from his classes as if they were labs, and his creation of communities of learners.

Thus while I have evidence that it is great teachers whom I have studied, I do not have records by which to evaluate how often or how long these great teachers produced great teaching. I do not consider that a terribly important issue. Each person selected meant something to me personally, and as I present them, they are useful in working through the particulars and the generalizations in developing an understanding of the distinctiveness of great teachers and great teaching.

I also argue that this book represents empirical research, if not in the obvious and traditional way, in a professionally defensible way. While much academic research is considered either quantitative or qualitative, a different epistemology has been recognized for the knowledge of practice. The contents of this book are very much steeped in "empiricism," more than thirty years of reflective practice, and based in the disciplined inquiry of working through the relationship of Peterson's description of great teachers with regard to the great teachers that I have had, have worked with, and have read about.

Another of my own recognized biases is why I distinguish great teachers from great teaching. The characteristic that I have added to Peterson's list is that a great teacher teaches to every student in her/his class. I was encouraged in reading Jay Mathews's book, *Work Hard. Be Nice.*, and then by him personally, to add this consideration to any discussion of great teachers. While I believe that those whom I have included meet all the characteristics described, all the evidence for my "conclusions" about these teachers is based in my limited experience and/or written records from one person's point of view and/or a teacher's reputation and/or that teacher's own written accounts. I would prefer to know what I cannot know—what was each and every student's experience of that teacher? The important reason: I would discount any teacher who only exhibited such qualities of great teaching for some select part of a class. I rankle at teachers who are recognized as great teachers, for example, who curried favor with a favored group of students but at the expense of other students.

Meanwhile, my study is substantiated by indicators that at least at some point in their teaching careers the teachers included herein gave evidence of great teaching and that only a great teacher could have done so. They need not have sustained great teaching at all times and places to be helpful to the reader/teacher who seeks to be one of the great teachers, however long that list of great teachers has been in history.

This book also has a regrettable and unintentional bias toward the study of college teachers. First, Houston Peterson's book on *Great Teachers* mostly included published accounts of college teachers, probably because the writers were fairly famous writers who could get published for choosing to write about their professors at primarily extremely well-known colleges.

Second, I did not have the good fortune of having, at least by the standards of this work, a great teacher until high school. That realization is certainly not because I do not think that great teaching is done in earlier school years. Quite the contrary. My daughter had a legendary great teacher in preschool at Malibu Presbyterian Church, Verne Riggle; a favorite elementary teacher, Kris Stewart; and a great middle school teacher, Gene Bream, who had been great in Santa Monica, California, and quickly reestablished himself as great at Malibu Junior High School.

Great teachers are found from preschool to graduate school, and I want this book to have something to say to any teacher at any level. Especially because I personally felt that to become a good teacher I needed to learn how to be effective at any level, so that whatever age I was teaching, I saw my students in the larger context of their full educational experience. Great teachers are needed as often as possible all along the way.

I began reading about teachers at the beginning of my career over forty years ago. If I had not personally had great elementary and middle school teachers, it only made me admire the Ashton-Warners, Kozols, Kohls, Holts, and Herndons all the more. I fully appreciate recent works about elementary school teachers Rafe Esquith and the KIPP teachers, and I have found great personal value in using the combination of my personal knowledge and experience of great teachers and the written records about great teachers. Nonetheless, I alert the reader that in my seeking to relate the general to the specific, my preschool through grade ten examples tend to come from books, and my grade eleven through PhD from personal experience.

A further limitation of my own background for the conduct of this study is a bias toward the humanities in contrast to math and the sciences. The KIPP teachers have had success teaching their students math, Escalante and Jimenez with calculus, but the preponderance of the teachers reviewed in this study were not for the most part from math or science. That certainly does not mean that I have any less respect for the possibilities of great teaching from math and science. In fact, the greatest teacher that I know personally, Larry Giacomino, teaches the sciences of chemistry, biology, and physics at the high school level. Neither is art nor music as represented, as I would have preferred.

This reality reminds me that I am in some ways a great teaching victim. Standardized test scores suggest that my academic strength would have been in mathematics. If an Escalante instead of a Daly had captured my educational imagination, I would certainly have had a very different school experience. However, I am not ruing that difference. What would have been more likely is that I would have left my school experience without having had any great teacher at all, and, thus, probably spent less time in school, and I certainly would not have become a teacher or eventually undertaken this book.

Thus, I do not apologize for the preponderance of attention to areas associated with the humanities, but I do acknowledge the limitation.

The list of great teachers also has a regrettable male bias. Sociograms done at professional conferences indicate that males tend to sit together while females do the same. Perhaps because of such social tendencies I have known more male rather than female teachers. In my school era many more professors were male. Males have more often written lives-in-teaching books. If historically men have been more likely to specialize, perhaps they have also been more willing to commit themselves to the excesses suggested by this book's criteria for greatness. The great personal and family costs associated with great teaching is by Aristotle's standards probably excessive, not meeting the golden mean of virtue. Rafe Esquith writes in some detail about the dangers of being obsessed with teaching. Whatever the reasons, this study had more males available for study.

While several ethnic groups are represented in the list of great teachers, and while their numbers are underrepresented on this list, for whatever reasons they are actually overrepresented in terms of how very few I had as teachers, perhaps more limited to the teaching profession by historic patterns of discrimination. While "prominence" has not been an equal opportunity employer, I have found no indication that anyone from any background might not be a great teacher.

OTHER PERSPECTIVES ON GREAT TEACHERS (AND THE ADVANTAGES OF THE PETERSON APPROACH)

Ken Bain (2004) studied sixty professors from various disciplines to determine "What Makes Great Teachers Great?" He asked the question: "What do any of the best professors do to encourage students to achieve remarkable learning results?" His answers include that they "create a natural learning environment." Bain argues that "by far the most important principle" for learning is that the teachers "ask probing and insightful questions." He details the relationship of the learning environment and posing questions:

> (1) An intriguing question or problem is the first of five essential elements that make up a good learning environment . . . guidance in helping students understand the (2) significance of the question . . . embed the discipline's issues in broader concerns, often taking an interdisciplinary approach . . . remind student how the current question relates to some large issue that already interests them . . . third . . . (3) engage students in some higher-order intellectual activity . . . fourth . . . (4) helps students themselves answer the question . . . (and) finally . . . (5) leaves students wondering: "What's the next question?" and "What can we ask now?"

Bain's tips include:

1. Get students' attention and keep it;
2. Start with the students rather than the discipline;
3. Seek commitments;
4. Help students learn outside of class . . . helps build a sense of community . . . encouraging students to learn on their own, engaging them in deep thinking;
5. Engage students in disciplinary thinking;
6. Create diverse learning experiences (Bain, 2004:B7).

As discussed more thoroughly in chapter 3, Bain's findings about what makes great teachers great rightly emphasizes the kind of questioning climate that great teachers surely create, but Bain overly confines his list of the ways he considers great teaching, and his observations tend to be more relevant to college teachers than K–12 teachers. Despite those limitations in regard to the purposes of this book, Bain shows courage in asserting that college professors should start with the students in their preparations instead of the discipline and in encouraging professors to diversify instruction. Within in his self-selected limitations, Bain's conclusions are consistent with Peterson's ideas about great teachers.

FOURTEEN THINGS THAT MATTER MOST FROM *WHAT GREAT TEACHERS DO DIFFERENTLY* BY TODD WHITAKER

1. Great teachers never forget that it is people, not programs, that determine the quality of a school.
2. Great teachers establish clear expectations at the start of the year and follow them consistently as the year progresses.
3. When a student misbehaves, great teachers have one goal: to keep that behavior from happening again.
4. Great teachers have high expectations for students but even higher expectations for themselves.
5. Great teachers know who is the variable in the classroom: they are. Good teachers consistently strive to improve, and they focus on something they can control—their own performance.
6. Great teachers create a positive atmosphere in their classrooms and schools. They treat every person with respect. In particular they understand the power of praise.
7. Great teachers consistently filter out negatives that don't matter and share a positive attitude.
8. Great teachers work hard to keep their relationships in good repair—to avoid personal hurt and to repair any possible damage.
9. Great teachers have the ability to ignore trivial disturbances and the ability to respond to inappropriate behavior without escalating the situation.
10. Great teachers have a plan and purpose for everything they do. If things don't work out the way they had envisioned, they reflect on what they could have done differently and adjust their plan accordingly.

11. Before making any decision or attempting to bring about any change, great teachers ask themselves one central question: What will the best people think?
12. Great teachers continually ask themselves who is most comfortable and who is least comfortable with each decision they make. They treat everyone as if they were good.
13. Great teachers keep standardized testing in perspective; they center on the real issue of student learning.
14. Great teachers care about their students. They understand that behaviors and beliefs are tied to emotion, and they understand the power of emotion to jump-start change.

Who would argue with Todd Whitaker's list of fourteen things that matter most? Perhaps most great teachers if discussing the list privately when candor might prevail over good manners. The list seems far too nice. Great teachers are aware of the many perils of great teaching, especially early-on complaints from students about the teacher being too hard and from administrators who might prefer the great teacher conform to the usual ways of doing things. Such great teachers might well complain that the list lacks the edgy qualities that come with achieving great teaching.

For example, "Great teachers never forget that it is people, not programs, that determine the quality of a school." That so goes without saying as to seem self-serving at best, unhelpful at worst. It may "matter," but this is not the sort of thing a great teacher thinks about. Do great teachers follow their preset expectations consistently? Nonsense. The great teacher uses the class as a lab, and thus knows that clear expectations set at the start of a year would tend to lead to inauthentic teaching.

That does not mean the great teacher does not have a full appreciation of the general expectations for a particular class. But so much of the important learning will emerge that early clarity would be a lie, and great teachers want their students to become more comfortable with ambiguity.

Great teachers are not overly worried about misbehavior; misbehavior is visible feedback (unlike passive resistance), so a great teacher would not want to focus on keeping such behavior from happening again, per se, only that it would happen in a different context, so that further feedback can be realized.

Do great teachers have even higher expectations for themselves? Of course, but they don't go around thinking in these terms. Are teachers the critical variable? The list reads too much like propaganda. A positive atmosphere? Sometimes an underachieving class needs harsh criticism (which when done by great teachers, the students will recognize that they need it in timely ways), and spoiled students have been found to need less praise and rather come to realize that praise is not cheaply given.

Great teachers will keep their relationships in good repair, but often by causing conflict with students that they then work through together. Including "trivial disturbances" in such a list trivializes the more important things that great teachers do. Great teachers may intuitively have a purpose for everything they do, but so much of it is intuitive that it seems superfluous to discuss it in these terms.

Great teachers are the best people, so they don't worry very much what anyone else might think. Comfort? Great teachers are not very concerned about comfort when it comes to teaching. Certainly great teachers do keep standardized testing in perspective and do care about their students and focus on being genuinely kind instead of superficially nice with students for whom they take such a keen interest in helping to a better life.

Perhaps these criticisms pose too strong of an objection to most of the items on this well-intentioned list. The purpose of the stridency is not so much to discredit any potential good of the list as to emphasize that great teachers tend to be very prickly when the conflict and complexities of teaching are neglected, and that great teachers protect their right to what Emerson refers to as the "rude word of truth."

The following is the Practical Theory List called What Makes a Great Teacher? at http://practicaltheory.org/serendipity/index.php?archives/8-What-makes=a-great-teacher.htm.

1. Passion for teaching.
2. Love of kids.
3. Love of their subject.
4. Understand the role of a school in a child's life.
5. A willingness to change.
6. A work ethic that doesn't quit.
7. A willingness to reflect.
8. Organization.
9. Understanding that being a "great teacher" is a constant struggle to improve.
10. Enough ego to survive the hard days.
11. Enough humility to remember it's not about you. It's about the kids.
12. A willingness to work collaboratively.

Who could disagree with the Practical Theory List on what makes a great teacher? Certainly the list is not inconsistent with Peterson's. However, one can read the list without necessarily thinking of what really makes teachers like the thirty-two of this study special, and the list's description of what "makes" a great teacher is more about what words describe a great teacher rather than revealing insight into how a great teacher got that way.

This list is from What Makes a Great Teacher? by the Great Schools staff at   http://www.greatschools.org/improvement/quality-teaching/79-what-makes-a-great-teacher.gs.

1. Great teachers set high expectations for all students.
2. Great teachers are prepared and organized.
3. Great teachers engage students and get them to look at issues in a variety of ways.
4. Great teachers form strong relationships with their students and show that they care about them as people.
5. Great teachers are masters of their subject matter.
6. Great teachers communicate frequently with parents.

The Great Schools staff indicate that great teachers are prepared and organized. Unfortunately what many mean by prepared and organized is not how great teachers are likely to think of preparation and organization. Great teachers are too busy to make lesson plans because they are too busy planning lessons. Research shows that seemingly well-planned lessons lead to ineffective and inauthentic teaching because such a teacher will try to force through the lesson instead of respond to the students. Organization schemes are often logical plans that might work for programming a computer but do not recognize (with John Dewey) the need for the psychological organization of the curriculum, so that learning activities evolve and come in the order in which they will be best received by the students.

Great teachers communicate with parents in whatever ways work for the students. Because of the necessity of students establishing their independence, which schools help them to do, frequent parental contact is not always what the student most needs. Finally, the list does not account for the ways great teachers became great; for example, by the tendency to see their classes as labs where they continually experiment to find what works with this particular group of students.

Claudia Wallis inquires into how to make great teachers, asking, "How do they come by their craft?" and saying that "it takes at least two years to master the basics of classroom management and six to seven years to become a fully proficient teacher." But her article becomes a discussion of merit pay and retention rather than a story of great teaching (2008:1, 3).

Of course, anyone can define great teaching however they like. The author prefers the Houston Peterson list of characteristics because it so aptly describes those teachers that he considers being great. Others can define great teaching by a different muse, but the differences in such imaginations of greatness may be instructive for further refining the sense of great teaching contained in this book.

Index

Half Moon Bay High School, 12, 73, 88
Hart, Leslie, 121
Hawkinshire, Frank, 5, 24, 26, 27, 35, 37,
    40, 63, 101, 107
Hecht, Anthony, 16
Herndon, Jim, 9, 16, 24, 25, 28, 38, 42, 48,
    53, 54, 88, 125, 146, 148
hidden curriculum, 31, 37, 38–39, 50
high standards, setting, 14, 16, 31, 33–34,
    45, 73, 109, 122, 128, 130
Holmes, David, 57, 88
Hook, Sidney, 32
How to Survive in Your Native Land
    (Herndon), 9
Hunter, Elizabeth, 80–82

Inchausti, Robert, 10, 25, 52, 88
intelligences, multiple, 69–70, 75

Jackson, Philip, 35, 38, 79
Jimenez, Ben, 10, 25, 27, 29, 37, 49, 34,
    57–59, 75, 88, 113, 119, 133, 144, 148
John Muir High School, 11
Joyce, Bruce, 76
Joyner, Florence, 72

Keeley, Jared, 88
Kingsfield, Professor, 11, 33
KIPP (Knowledge is Power Program), 9,
    10, 11, 27, 31, 32, 36, 43, 45, 47, 48,
    57, 88, 113, 145, 148
knowledge of students, 15, 16, 51,
    119–120, 123, 129
Kohl, Herbert, 43, 146, 148
Kozol, Jonathan, 53, 146, 148

laboratory, class as, 7, 9, 31, 33, 39–40, 41,
    42, 46, 56, 65, 72, 73, 75, 83, 88, 132,
    146, 151, 153
Ladson-Billings, 9, 25
learning community: creating expectations
    and common purpose, 44–45;
    appreciation, trust, truth, 45–46; time
    on what needed, 47; larger context,
    48–49
Leon, Nick, 48
Levin, Dave, 10, 11, 25, 32, 37, 45, 49, 57,
    66, 67, 88, 113
Levin, Hank, 67

Liesveld, Roseanne, 3, 4, 13
Live at Montreaux, 78

Machiavelli, Niccolo, 44
Malibu Park Junior High School, 147
Masters: Portraits of Great Teachers
    (Epstein), 16, 32, 36, 42, 60, 114
Mathews, Jay, 10–11, 16, 31, 32, 33, 36,
    39, 42, 43, 44, 45, 47, 48, 57–59, 119,
    133, 147
McCann, Les, 78, 79
McLellan, Jeffrey, 67
McGoldrick, Jim, 63
McGraw, Ali, 47
Miller, Jo Ann, 3, 4, 13
Miller, John William, 16, 42
Mission Bay High School, 5, 29, 46, 144
Morgan, Norah, 112
Mystic Pizza, 16

Nisbet, Robert, 60, 114
Noman, 38, 85, 88, 116, 125
Notes from the Classroom (Herndon), 9

Occidental College, 5, 25, 54
O'Hair, Mary John, 71
Olmos, James Earl, 3, 10, 26
On Education (Tolstoy), 16, 41
Overfelt High School, 57
Owen, Lewis, 5, 7, 24, 25, 27, 34, 37, 60,
    88, 114

Pacheco, Arturo, 6, 24, 27, 28, 37, 88, 107,
    146
Paper Chase, 11, 33, 55
Park, Charles Chang, 11, 24
Parsons, Talcott, 120–122
Pascarelli, Ernest, 66
Pawnbroker, 78
Pearce, Professor, 54
Pedagogy of the Oppressed (Freire), 9, 27
Pepperdine University, 5, 8, 9, 11, 16, 24
Persona of the great teacher, 34–37
personal characteristics of great teachers:
    #1 no fear, 14, 16, 25, 56; #2 thorough
    knowledge, 14, 16, 56; #3 rich fund of
    examples, 14, 16, 25, 128; #4 "best, 14,
    16, 25, 128; #5 challenging, 14, 16,
    128; #6 persona, 14, 16, 128; #7